¡Caliente Quilts!

Create Breathtaking Quilts
Using Bold Colors

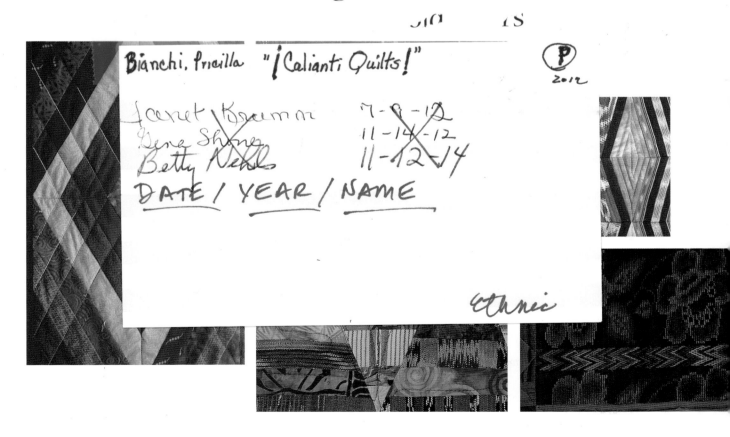

Bianchi, Priscilla   "¡Calianti Quilts!"   Ⓟ 2012

Janet Kramm   7-9-12

Gene Shore   11-14-12

Betty Nehls   11-12-14

DATE / YEAR / NAME

Ethnic

BY PRISCILLA BIANCHI

©2007 by Priscilla Bianchi

Published by

700 East State Street • Iola, WI 54990-0001
715-445-2214 • 888-457-2873
www.krausebooks.com

Our toll-free number to place an order or obtain a free catalog is (800) 258-0929.

The following trademarked terms and companies appear in this publication:
3M Fabric Grabbers®, Big Foot®, Energizer Bunny®, Little Foot®,
Quilter's Rule®, Retayne™, Singer®

Library of Congress Control Number: 2006935440

ISBN-13: 978-0-89689-383-2
ISBN-10: 0-89689-383-9

Designed by Sharon Bartsch and Katrina Newby
Edited by Erica Swanson and Margrit Hall

Printed in China

Dedication

To God, for all His many blessings, and for opening doors and making it all possible.

To my maternal grandmother, Mamita: You believed in me more than I did and always accepted me as I am. You instilled in me a passion for color and fabric, and an appreciation for fine needlearts in all forms.

To my parents: You provided opportunities for me to learn and grow as a person, and helped me realize my potential, believing that I am capable of doing anything. You offered unconditional love and support in so many ways, and you taught me to work hard, be productive and enjoy the satisfaction of a job well done.

To Mama: By teaching me to love art and see the beauty around me, you have given me a lifetime of enjoyment. By teaching me to sew, you opened up a world of possibilities.

To Papa: Thank you for your wonderful humor, your optimism and your positive outlook on life, no matter what. You are my rock.

To my aunts, Elisa, Tillie, Marta, Margarita, Elsie, Margot, Angelina and Beatriz: You have all been wonderful role models of independent, capable, decisive, strong women. You speak your mind and do not let anything or anyone bring you down. Thank you for teaching me to live life to the fullest and grow old gracefully.

To my brothers, Billy, Rodolfo, Gerardo, and Rolando: Thank you for your loving friendship and always being there when I need you. You taught me to stand up for myself; and you gave me so many memories of teasing and the laughter.

To my son Rodrigo: Thank you for your sound artistic advice that always manages to get me unstuck, your practical sense, and your unconditional love and support.

To my goddaughter Pamela: Thank you for your sweet companionship, and for bringing joy and lots of giggles into my life.

To my cousins, uncles, sisters-in-law, nieces and nephews: I am grateful for the camaraderie, the laughter and the good times we enjoy together.

Thank you all for teaching me to not take my life or myself too seriously, and to enjoy life's simple pleasures every day. Thanks for always rooting for me, and for your interest and admiration. My life is richer and better because of you all; I love you very much.

Acknowledgments

This book would not have been possible without input and assistance from the following people:

Candy Wiza, acquisitions editor, for your expertise and support that always managed to put my mind at ease.

My editor, Erica Swanson, and all the people at Krause Publications.

Margrit Hall, for developing/writing most of the projects in this book at the drop of a hat — and for all the last minute requests...

To Rosario Miralbés de Polanco and Barbara de Arathoon for sharing your knowledge and expertise about Mayan textiles of Guatemala, thus giving the book its spirit.

Bob Best and Kris Kandler, the photographers.

Sharon Bartsch and Katrina Newby, the book designers.

Jeff Labanz, Alan Benchoam, Pamela Cerezo and Rolando Bianchi, for providing the stunning photographs that show my beautiful Guatemala in all its glory.

David Lorenz, for inspiring me with your magnificent photography.

Ursula Newman, Jan Magee and Jan Krentz, for providing quality photos of my work.

The students in my classes, who keep me going with their genuine enthusiasm and interest; you take my ideas and run with them in all sorts of directions that I never would have imagined! You teach me so much!

My mentors, colleagues, associates, sponsors and friends in the quilting world, who have welcomed me with open hearts and minds, who have given me encouragement and guidance along the way, and who have opened doors and presented opportunities for me to advance.... I thank you all more than words can say!

The Maya people of Guatemala, for their cultural diversity and textile heritage that inspire me every single day of my life.

To all textile craftsmen and artisans around the world, who have given us such wonderful heritages to enjoy and expand.

Table of Contents

Introduction

This book is for you if:

1. You have admired exotic or outrageous fabrics in the past, but you have no idea what to do with them.

2. You have been collecting unique fabrics that you unfold every now and then, caress, and put away because you don't have the courage to start cutting them up.

3. You want to expand your creative horizons, stretch out of your comfort zone and create original designs of your own.

4. You need a jumpstart — you want to become inspired and excited about making quilts again.

"Caliente Quilts" has the answer! Grab those gorgeous goodies and get ready for some guilt-free, passion-driven, fearless fun! I am uniquely qualified to guide you on your creative journey because I am a native Guatemalan quilt artist, designer and international teacher. My own voyage of discovery — merging the traditional Euro-American craft of quilting with the unique textiles of my country and other exotic textiles from around the world — has been an incredible, life-changing experience. Mom said to me just the other day, "Prisci, did you ever imagine that knowing how to sew would take you around the world?" I could not have possibly imagined the many wonderful things that have happened in the past eight years. The fantastic opportunities that I have been given, the places I have been, the extraordinary people I have met and friends I have made, and the fact that I am writing these words — it is all amazing! I work very hard, but I have also been extremely lucky. I have learned a lot and grown in every aspect of my life, and I am elated to be sharing it all with you.

When I walked into New York's American Craft Museum in 2002 and saw one of my quilts hanging side by side with a Nancy Crow quilt, my jaw

Here I am, posing in front of my quilt (and Nancy Crow's), enjoying my 15 minutes of fame!

dropped to the floor. What an experience! "Here I am," I thought, "and I didn't make my first quilt until five years ago, when I was forty-two."

LEFT: It doesn't get any better than this!
BELOW: Here I am, two years old, with my brother Rodolfo, five. Mom would dress us in typical costumes every year to celebrate the day of the Virgin of Guadalupe, December 12th.

I have been surrounded by needlework all my life in Guatemala, a country famous for its textiles. My mother taught me to sew on a Singer treadle sewing machine when I was four. My maternal grandmother taught me knitting (her main hobby) and crochet, and instilled in me a passion for color, fabrics and yarns; she was a fabricaholic! When I was eleven, my mother enrolled me in a dressmaking class, and from then on I sewed my own clothes; I have been creating and designing ever since.

RIGHT: At 23, I was already wearing a huipil, a traditional Maya blouse. Everything that has happened in my life has brought me to the point where I am now; I have loved Mayan textiles all my life!

My maternal grandmother, Mamita, who came with her parents from Barcelona, Spain, when she was five years old, loved to wear huipiles for special occasions. She would adorn them with "chachales," traditional necklaces made from antique coins (pesos) and silver charms. She thrived on color!

But we were not a typical Guatemalan family. My fraternal aunts grew up in California and became very Americanized. What a culture shock when they returned to Guatemala in 1933! Here, women were (and still are) generally submissive, dependent and subject to a lot of "machismo." My American-bred aunts were liberated women who had jobs, managed their own money, drove cars and spoke their minds. They were excellent role models for us, the younger generation.

This cultural fusion led to my interest in quilting. When the excitement of my career in industrial psychology began to fade, I started to look for new outside interests. Quilting had been at the back of my mind for many years, but I never had time to pursue it. The books I found made it look very complicated. Then in 1997, I found *Charm Quilts* by Beth Donaldson. I read it in a day and immediately started my first quilt. I couldn't wait to finish it so I could do my second — and third! I was hooked!

One year later, I had finished thirty quilts, while still working nine-to-five. I had the tremendous advantage of full-time household help, something very common in Guatemala (when I mention this to American quilters, they usually say, "Oh, so that's your secret!"

LEFT: The very first two quilts I ever made were done in a frenzy! I could not finish them fast enough so I could get 'em out of the way and start on the next ones! "Four Color Pinwheel" (32" x 32") and "Which Came First?" (32" x 32")

and feel better). Still, I was a veritable Energizer Bunny, staying up until well after midnight each night. Then in 1999, I made a shocking decision; I retired and started quilting full-time. I knew I wanted to do this for the rest of my life, and I would have to give it my full, undivided attention.

ABOVE: My studio keeps creeping in on me. It has practically taken over the whole second floor of the house! I play and spend hours on end here.

Art quilting combines everything that I love! I'm a visual person, and I constantly draw inspiration and design ideas from all around me. The pattern on a manhole cover in Dromana, Australia is as exciting as the geometric shapes on an upholstered chair in Pacific Grove, California. I have always had an artistic streak; I sketch, draw and design continually and I love colors. I am passionate about fabric, both buying it and working with it. For me, finding a great fabric is an adrenaline rush, and I just "gotta have it!" I am curious and restless, so I experiment and try out new things continually. Art quilting puts all of my favorite things together in a fantastic package — what more could I ask for?

Guatemala has one of the richest textile traditions in the world, but since quilting is not part of our inherited Spanish culture, the quilting movement has not caught on here yet. In fact, I may be the entire quilting community! I have had to overcome many obstacles: no one to teach me, no support groups, no reference, no true quilting shops, books or notions. Yet, despite all the challenges, I've made more than 125 art quilts and had 22 solo shows to date in the U.S., Guatemala, Canada, Australia and France.

When I first started out, I knew that I could not be a traditional quilter since I had never had direct experience with quilts and I do not come from a quilting culture. I regretted not having a family quilting background. It seemed a great loss. Then I met Robert Shaw who was the curator of Quilts, Inc. at the time. He was impressed by my work and appreciative of how distinctive my art quilts were. He advised me to continue to seek inspiration within my own culture; he told me "not to look at quilts." That is when I realized that living abroad was a great advantage! Not being constantly bombarded and influenced by mainstream quilting shows, classes, shops and books was precisely what made me different, and different was good. I had no boundaries; I could do as I pleased!

Panoramic view of my very first solo show at the Ixchel Museum of Indigenous Dress in Guatemala City, Guatemala. March, 1999

At about that time I also encountered members of the "Quilt Police," experts who insist that things must be done only one way — their way. How fortunate I am to be free of that! I am not expected to do things in any certain way, so I have no limitations. I can experiment and try out a lot of new things. No one is peering over my shoulder, criticizing the creative or experimental things I am doing "wrong." Ignorance is daring!

My work is a marriage made in heaven; it is a transcendent fusion of cultures. American quilting techniques and patterns are combined with my own native Guatemalan designs and textiles, many of which are ancient Mayan in origin. For added variety and visual interest, I add to the mix other fabrics that share the same rustic, primitive, handmade qualities and complement each other in a most effective way. Indonesian batiks, African cloth, hand-dyed and hand-painted cottons, indigos, shibori, and yukatas mix to create a truly divine (pun intended) combination!

Finding the art of quilting has given my spirit an outlet to express itself and given meaning to my life. I'm sleepless many nights because of all the ideas, forms and colors dancing in my mind. The best creative solutions usually come to me in the wee hours of the morning.

I believe that art is a journey, and my quilts are pieces in a never-ending learning adventure toward a higher level of self-expression and spirituality. It's not the destiny, but the process that makes everything I do worthwhile.

I hope you enjoy my work as much as I enjoyed creating it. Now, let's dive in wholeheartedly!

Panoramic view of Priscilla's latest solo show at the National Museum of Modern Art "Carlos Mérida" in Guatemala City, Guatemala. April, 2006

Best regards!
Priscilla

Chapter 1
Sources of
Inspiration

Guatemala's land and people, with an inherited Spanish culture infused with the Maya soul and spirit, offer a rich scope for quilting. The land has a magical and uniquely mystical cultural diversity, and the people's fantastic energy and zest for life is expressed through multicolored costumes, traditional folk celebrations and rich visual imagery.

The Landscape

Guatemala is known as "The Land of Eternal Spring" for its pleasant, mild climate all year round. Here, nature plays with color in an awe-inspiring palette, with blue sapphire lakes, green emerald mountains and a fiery coral sunset sky. Such breathtaking beauty steals your heart away!

TOP: The sunset in Poptún can be a fiery red. *Photo, Alan Benchoam.*
ABOVE LEFT: The summer sky at sunset is glorious. *Photo, Jeff Labanz.*
ABOVE RIGHT: Looking down on the highland mountains, you can see crops in every conceivable shade of green. *Photo, Jeff Labanz.*
LEFT: Men carry wood the old-fashioned way near Lake Atitlán. *Photo, Alan Benchoam.*

LEFT: Visit Quiriguá to see ancient Mayan temples in all their splendor. *Photo, Jeff Labanz.*

BELOW LEFT: People grow cauliflowers in the fertile land of "Tierra Fría" (Cold Land), as the highlands are called. *Photo, Jeff Labanz.*

BELOW RIGHT: The northern rainforest with its thick jungle offers a very different land-scape in a very hot climate. It is refreshing to find a cascade like this! *Photo, Jeff Labanz.*

ABOVE: The topography of the Mayan towns in the highlands is very distinctive and picturesque. *Photo, Jeff Labanz.*

Colonial Architecture

45 minutes away from Guatemala City lies the enchanting, romantic, city of Antigua. Here, you will enter a fascinating world reminiscent of the 16th century with cobblestone streets, fountains, baroque-style architecture and charming courtyards with blooming gardens. The city is a silent witness to Antigua's glorious past.

Destroyed by an earthquake in 1773, Antigua's ruins have been restored and preserved as a testament to a bygone era. Stunning examples of colonial architecture are found in the intricately detailed church façades, the many convents' ruins, captivating archways and private mansions. Antigua exudes the unique energy of a city where past and present live in perfect harmony.

ABOVE LEFT AND RIGHT: The magnificent central courtyard and archways at Las Capuchinas ruins in Antigua, Guatemala. Exuberant bougainvilleas flower in February and November. *Photo, Jeff Labanz.*

ABOVE: This archway takes you to one of the courtyards at the ruins of La Recolección Convent, Antigua, Guatemala. *Photo, Jeff Labanz.*

RIGHT: In front of the atrium of the Cathedral in Antigua, men hurriedly finish a sawdust rug so it will be ready in time for the approaching procession. *Photo, Alan Benchoam.*

TOP: One of the communal "pilas" in Antigua, which are essential for social interaction. This is where women gather every day to wash clothes and hear the latest scoop. *Photo, Alan Benchoam.*

ABOVE LEFT: Clay tiles and domed ceilings at Castillo de San Felipe, on Guatemala's Atlantic coast. The fort was built to guard the local inhabitants from pirate incursions. *Photo, Jeff Labanz.*

ABOVE RIGHT: Breathtaking panoramic view of the city of Antigua, from the nearby Cerro de la Cruz (Mount of the Cross). *Photo, Jeff Labanz.*

RIGHT: A spectacular example of Colonial architecture at its best. The deep blue sky provides a fitting backdrop for the magnificent lines and features of the dome. *Photo, Jeff Labanz.*

Imagery

Visitors who come to Guatemala for the first time are in awe of the visual imagery that abounds everywhere: Here there are weathered walls, religious processions, folk festivals, church façades and symbols of the cross, all of which describe the people's rich cultural diversity. The rituals, traditions and teachings passed on by Mayan and Spanish ancestors are an essential part of the lifestyle of today's native population.

There is an underlying mystical energy in Guatemala that is very attractive. In this fascinating world, indigenous beliefs merge with Catholic rituals, yielding infinite images of masks, costumes, religious ceremonies and dances. You can feel the very heart of the land itself.

LEFT: I have seen these images ever since I can remember. The fact that "purple is the color of Holy Week" is so ingrained in me that it appears time and time again in my work. The men, dressed in formal purple attire, are in penitence and mourning to commemorate the passion of Christ. *Photo, Jeff Labanz.*

BELOW: A man in purple, or "cucurucho" as we call them, is on his way to a procession. What a beautiful naturally-distressed textured wall! I cannot help but notice that these two colors are complementary. *Photo, Alan Benchoam.*

BELOW: This scene, with hundreds of lit candles glowing inside the Cathedral, is spiritual and holy. People light candles to worship God and ask Him for His help and mercy. Cobán, Alta Verapaz. *Photo, Alan Benchoam.*

BELOW: Even the cemetery is multicolored! The beautiful cemetery of Chichicastenango sits quietly atop a small hill overlooking the town. *Photo, Jeff Labanz.*

BELOW MIDDLE: The traffic in Guatemala City is singular. This is the spirit of my improvisational work, which is a free-form, organized disorder! *Photo, Jeff Labanz.*

ABOVE: Rugs for processions are usually made of dyed sawdust or fresh flowers. This rug, made from ceremonial blouses and cloth, is extremely unusual. It certainly grabbed my attention! *Photo, Jeff Labanz.*

The Marketplace

Markets in Guatemala are alive with sounds, sights, smells and flavors that appeal and excite the senses. Going to the open markets immerses you in today's Mayan spirit. Fruits and vegetables, pine furniture, silver, ceramics, needles and threads, incense, textiles — everything you need is for sale.

Color, of course, is present at the market. It has been said that Guatemalans need color as air to breathe! And it is absolutely true; just as the Maya wear costumes as colorful as the rainbow, the market offers every imaginable hue in the universe.

LEFT: Man in Antigua, displaying huipiles and other textiles for sale. What a sight — an authentic sea of cloth! *Photo, Alan Benchoam.*
BELOW: Multicolored chilis for sale at the market. *Photo, Alan Benchoam.*
BOTTOM: Young woman in Panajachel, Sololá selling woolen bags ("morrales") and other arts and crafts. I love the textured adobe wall! *Photo, Alan Benchoam.*

LEFT: The busy flower market on the steps of Santo Tomás church in Chichicastenango. *Photo, Alan Benchoam.*
BELOW: Is there a color you don't have? Fabric bags for sale at the crafts market in Antigua. *Photo, Jeff Labanz.*

ABOVE: Gorgeous textiles of all kinds, sizes and shapes are found everywhere! Strikingly beautiful, hand-woven multicolored striped sashes. *Photo, Jeff Labanz.*
RIGHT: Wooden masks of every color, shape and character imaginable! *Photo, Jeff Labanz.*

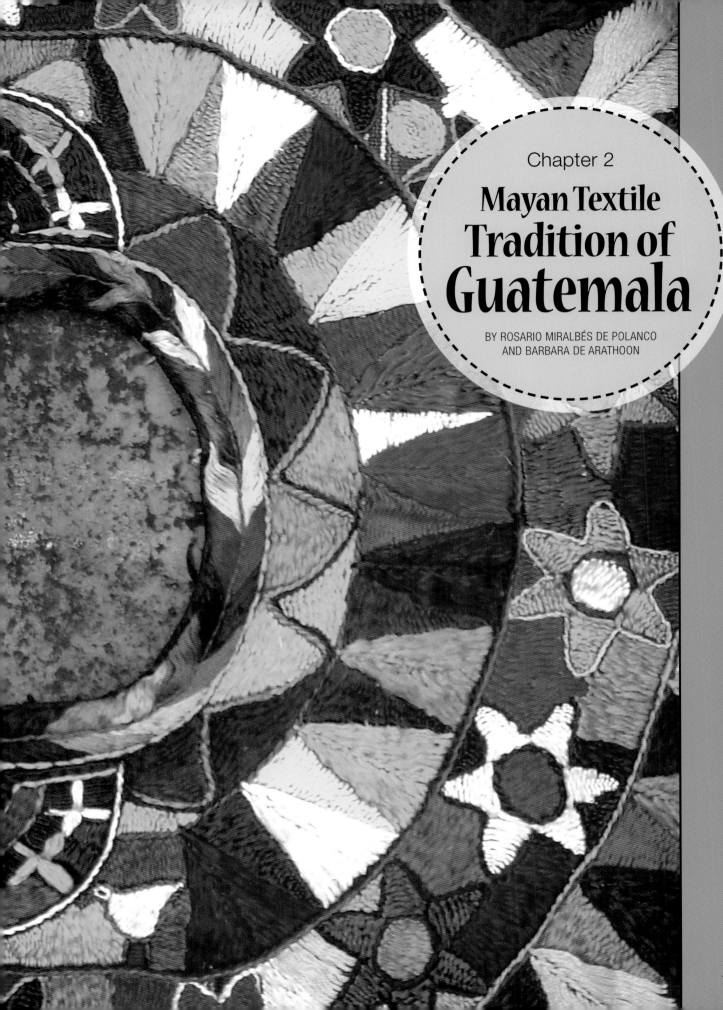

Chapter 2
Mayan Textile
Tradition of
Guatemala

BY ROSARIO MIRALBÉS DE POLANCO
AND BARBARA DE ARATHOON

Guatemala, a small country (67,632 miles) located in Central America, embraces within its varied geography great cultural and linguistic diversity. The majority of its population is comprised within two main ethnic groups: indigenous people and Ladinos (part-Spanish, part-indigenous). The majority of the indigenous population, more than five and a half million people, continues to speak 21 different Mayan languages. They have also preserved other important expressions of their identity, like a particular vision of the world and a remarkable textile tradition which threads their history together.

LEFT: Map showing Guatemala's location in the center of the American continent. *Courtesy of Editorial Piedra Santa, Guatemala.*
BELOW: Opening the door to the living Mayan culture of Guatemala. *Photo, Alan Benchoam.*

Maya civilization, which also occupied parts of Mexico, Belize, El Salvador and Honduras, dates back to 1500 B.C. It flourished during what's known as the "classic period" (250 – 900 A.D.), a time during which great advances were made in mathematics, glyphic writing, astronomy and time recording. The arts and monumental architecture also reached higher levels of refinement, all based on a profoundly religious conception of life and the world. Their clothing's richness and variety reflected the fact that rituals were an essential part of life for the ruling elite.

Over 3,500 years ago, the Maya established themselves in Central America and built monumental cities that revolved around a profoundly religious concept of the world. *Photo Quiriguá by Jeff Labanz.*

The Maya sculpted colossal stelaes where they documented their life and dress. *Photo Quiriguá by Jeff Labanz.*

Ancient textile techniques included spinning cotton and agave fibers (century plant, sisal and hemp), dyeing, printing and weaving. Archaeological evidence indicates that several methods for interweaving warp (vertical threads) and weft (horizontal threads) were known including plain weave, tapestry and gauze weave. Supplementary wefts were added to obtain decorative motifs, or brocades. Mayan weavers had attained a high level of technical skill on the backstrap loom, which was used to weave garments such as "huipiles" (blouses), "cortes" (wraparound skirts), head dresses, sashes, loincloths, hip-cloths, capes, vests, ceremonial cloths and more.

ABOVE LEFT: Nets and ropes made from agave fibers on sale at the open market. ©*Photo Anne Girard, 2003, courtesy of The Ixchel Museum of Indigenous Dress, Guatemala.*
ABOVE RIGHT: Fine gauze weave from Cobán, Alta Verapaz, depicting human and animal figures.

Descendants of the ancient Mayas kept their culture alive for several centuries before the arrival of the Spaniards in 1524. Nevertheless, the conquest and subsequent colonization dramatically transformed them. These changes were echoed in the textile tradition which began to include new materials (silk and wool) and instruments (treadle loom), as well as different styles of clothing (ruffled skirts, mantles, wool trousers and jackets). Traditional pre-Hispanic and colonial styles are still worn today, in addition to newly-developed modern styles.

Nowadays, traditional Mayan clothing, known as "traje," retains distinctive characteristics which identify the wearer's community of origin; among these characteristics are the garment's color, designs, style and mode of use, as well as the techniques employed to make them. Within this type of dress, one finds everyday clothing and ceremonial garments worn by "cofradía" (religious organizations) members.

ABOVE: Woman wearing her distinctive Mayan everyday clothing, or "traje," from Todos Santos Cuchumatán, Huehuetenango. She uses her fringed shawl to strap the little girl on her back. *©Photo by Danielle Reveney, courtesy of The Ixchel Museum of Indigenous Dress, Guatemala.*

ABOVE: Religious leaders or, "cofrades," from Chichicastenango in full ceremonial dress that denotes their rank and status. Their elegant apparel includes an embroidered wool jacket and pants, black wool overcoat (capixay) and headwrap (su't). *Photo, Alan Benchoam.*

Beginning in the 1970s, Mayan communities were transformed by incessant changes. Soon thereafter modern-style clothing began to appear, breaking away from traditional codes.

Men's Clothing

There are relatively few men who continue to wear traditional everyday clothing styles, and most of those that do live in the highlands. Men's clothing is usually woven and made by women. It consists of a shirt, trousers, belt or sash, "su't" (multi-purpose cloth) and hat. Other wool garments that are either made or purchased include: overtrousers, jacket, "capixay" (overcoat) and "rodilleras" (wrap-around apron-like cloth). The disappearance of the majority of traditional men's clothing is likely due to the fact that men have had more contact with the outside world. They migrate to the south coast during harvest season, search for employment in the city, or do business with neighboring communities.

ABOVE LEFT: Man wearing his distinctive traje from San Pedro La Laguna, Sololá. Notice all the components of the costume: pants, shirt, sash, additional leather belt, woolen jacket, hat and woolen bag known as "morral." ©*Photo Anne Girard, 1970, courtesy of The Ixchel Museum of Indigenous Dress, Guatemala.*
ABOVE CENTER: Knitted and crocheted woolen bags (morrales) are part of men's costumes in many highland towns.
ABOVE RIGHT: Self-assured young boy wearing his distinctive Mayan everyday "traje" from Todos Santos Cuchumatán, Huehuetenango. The shirt's long extended collar, the black woolen overtrousers and the multicolored tapestry crocheted bag are unique to this town. It is interesting to note the addition of a western bandana to complement the costume. ©*Photo by Danielle Reveney, courtesy of The Ixchel Museum of Indigenous Dress, Guatemala.*

LEFT: While the two girls wear the traditional dress from their village, Santa Catarina Palopó, Sololá, the little boy is already wearing a western-style T-shirt and pants.
Photo, Alan Benchoam.

Religious leaders known as cofrades wear special ritual and ceremonial clothing that denotes their rank and status. This clothing tends to be rich and often quite complex. The number of garments used on these occasions differs from one community to another; some simply wear a sash and others a complete outfit.

RIGHT: Members of the cofradía of Sololá and San Juan Sacatepéquez respectively, carrying their scepters and proudly displaying their status as religious leaders of the community. *Photo, Anne Girard, courtesy of The Ixchel Museum of Indigenous Dress, Guatemala. Photo, Edwin Castro, courtesy of The Ixchel Museum of Indigenous Dress, Guatemala.*

Women's Clothing

Most of the communities that still wear traditional everyday traje, distinctively identifying the wearer's origin, are found in Guatemala's highland region. The women's garments generally include: a huipil (blouse), skirt, sash, one or more su'ts (multi-purpose cloths), shawl, apron and a decorative element worn on the head (head dress). The huipil bears the most elements of identity. It is made of one, two or three panels and hand-woven mainly on backstrap looms. Today, only the elder women in the community continue to wear this style of clothing in the same way their ancestors did. Younger women have varied the color and size of the figures decorating their huipiles.

ABOVE: Old woman from Santa Cruz La Laguna, Sololá. Embellishing the traditional costume with necklaces of different types is customary. *Photo, Alan Benchoam.*

FAR LEFT: Young woman from San Pedro Sacatepéquez, Guatemala. *Photo by Maria Luisa Schlesinger, courtesy of The Lachel Museum of Indigenous Dress, Guatemala.*

LEFT: Women from the Cofradía of San Juan Sacatepéquez carrying flower offerings during a religious procession. *Photo by Edwin Castro, courtesy of The Ixchel Museum of Indigenous Dress, Guatemala.*

Women who belong to the cofradía wear distinguishing ceremonial attire that denotes their hierarchy and social standing. Communities differ in the way these are worn. Garments and cloths used for ceremonial purposes generally include an overblouse, veil, head ribbon, paños (square cloths) of several sizes to wrap candles or offerings, handkerchiefs and napkins. For the most part, these ceremonial textiles are hand-woven with finer materials and complex techniques to show economic status.

Modern Women's Clothing

The "regional" style of clothing no longer has the specific traits of a particular community, but it retains common characteristics to a region. This style has developed in areas with a greater degree of acculturation, where women wear traditional-shaped huipiles made from commercial cloth along with jaspe (ikat) skirts.

The "generalized" style serves to identify Guatemala's Mayan women in general, but no longer transmits the codes present in traditional clothing styles, e.g. the wearer's place of origin, social and religious position, and marital status. This style includes basic garments like: a blouse constructed as a huipil but made of commercial cloth which may be then hand or machine embroidered. In most cases, a jaspe skirt, sash, shawl or sweater, and apron are also worn.

In many highland communities and in the cities, young professional women wear other types of indigenous clothing. These are difficult to specify among the different styles, so anthropologists refer to them as "pan-Maya." This style differs from the "generalized" because it includes garments that are clearly recognized as distinctive from a certain community, but are combined with others that have more regional or general characteristics, mainly the jaspe skirt. They may wear complete trajes that are not from their communities of origin.

ABOVE: Regional trajes from the area of Alta Verapaz, in the northern central part of the country. Although shaped in the traditional style, the blouses are made from commercial fabric. *Photos by Anne Girard, courtesy of The Ixchel Museum of Indigenous Dress, Guatemala.*
RIGHT: Detail of the regional blouse with modern-style embroidery over commercial cloth.

During the last few decades, Guatemala has gone through a series of economic, cultural, social and political changes that affected the life of Mayan communities and thus generated identity changes. A 36-year civil war (1960 – 1996), which ended with the signing of Peace Treaties, and the appearance of the Maya revival movement in 1990 caused upheaval. Today, many women express a sense of pride and ethnic sisterhood which extends beyond their municipalities of origin, which is evident in their use of "pan-Maya" clothing. Entrepreneurs, merchants and political leaders who have adopted this style design their clothing using distinctive elements from different communities according to their own personal preferences, and not according to tradition anymore.

Designs and Symbolism

Maya clothing boasts complex ornamentation like horizontal and vertical stripes, geometric or figurative designs, or a combination of these elements. The chromatic impact and technical complexity of these designs are integral to the clothing. Among these decorative motifs are flowers, trees and animals such as monkeys, jaguars, horses, squirrels, rabbits and deer. Some of them are actually symbols that contain messages alluding to the traditional Maya vision of the cosmos. In certain communities, zigzags and diamonds refer to serpents and stars, respectively. Birds such as eagles, turkeys, chickens, hens, parrots and parakeets are depicted often and sometimes refer to characters found in legends. The decorative motifs around the collar represent the sun and the moon in some cases, and in others, volcanoes.

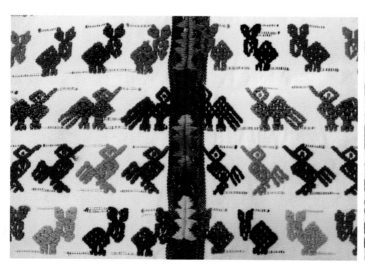

ABOVE: This huipil from San Pedro Sacatepéquez displays a variety of animal figures.
ABOVE RIGHT: This huipil from Santiago Atitlán contains interesting symbolism; the hole for the head represents the Lake while the embroidered adornment around the neck represents the volcanoes. *Photo, Anne Girard, courtesy of the Ixchel Museum of Indigenous Dress, Guatemala.*
RIGHT: Lake Atitlán surrounded by imposing volcanoes. *Photo, Alan Benchoam.*

In some communities, the distinctive symbols used to adorn cofradía and wedding ceremonial blouses include a dead turkey and the tree of life. Although their visual shapes appear to have been introduced by the Spaniards, their meanings have pre-Columbian roots. The dead turkey represents a ritual offering given by the groom's family to his future in-laws on the day of the wedding. The tree of life symbolizes the woman as the giver of life; its branches are her children.

ABOVE: The dead turkey symbol. *Photo, Anne Girard, courtesy The Ixchel Museum of Indigenous Dress, Guatemala.*
RIGHT: The tree of life symbol.

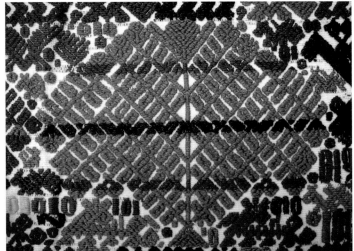

In recent decades, copying decorative flowers, fruits and birds from cross-stitch magazines has become a fashionable trend. Communities will trade these motifs among them, due to their attractive look and the prestige that comes from rendering designs that require such high technical skill.

Two striking examples of decorative motifs copied from cross-stitch magazines.

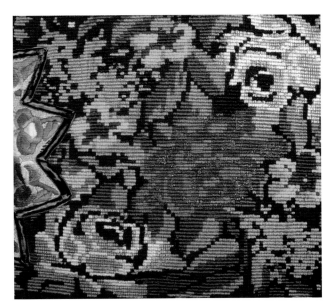

Materials, Techniques and Procedures

Since ancient times, Mayan women have produced clothing for themselves and their families, passing on the textile tradition knowledge from one generation to the next. As mothers and grandmothers have interwoven their skill, artistry, customs and techniques, they have also ensured the survival of the exceptional Mayan textile tradition. Weaving is a complex process that requires great skill in handling many different tools and knowledge of diverse materials. Some of these are pre-Hispanic in origin and others were introduced during the colonial period (1524 – 1821). Technical advances initiated in Europe in the fourteenth century had an impact on Mayan weaving as well.

Cofrades from Quetzaltenango in formal dress. Circa 1900 *Photo courtesy The Ixchel Museum of Indigenous Dress, Guatemala.*

Materials

Before the Spanish conquest, the Maya used white cotton and natural brown-colored cotton fibers which they spun by hand into thread using a spindle. Although there is no physical evidence to support the claim that the Maya used animal fibers, colonial-era chroniclers report the use of wild silk and certain animal hairs, such as rabbit.

Hand-spinning threads is a tedious process which became widespread during the colonial period. In addition to spinning thread for their own use, women were required to produce large amounts of thread to pay as tribute to the colonizers. Upon their arrival to Guatemala, the Spaniards introduced silk and sheep's wool. Indigenous people adopted these materials to make certain garments. Although the tradition of spinning by hand has been almost lost, some women continue to produce natural brown-colored cotton thread for weaving ceremonial garments. Spinning wool with the spinning wheel, also introduced by the Spaniards, is still practiced in the cooler regions of the country's western departments.

It is common to find multicolored threads for sale at the open market. *Photo, Jeff Labanz.*

Industrially-spun threads and chemical dyes were introduced at the end of the 19th century; soon after rayon followed. Synthetic fibers like nylon and later polyester, which were to revolutionize weaving throughout the world, first arrived in the country at the end of the 1930s. During the mid 1960s, acrylic fibers became popular, and their use quickly transformed the color palette of indigenous clothing.

Dyeing

The process of dyeing threads is particularly interesting, evoking mysteries related to cultural symbolism and social hierarchies. For example, body painting was common in the ancient Maya culture and had different connotations. Colonial documents report that indigenous men were good with dyes and wore colored clothing; they especially mention blue dye obtained from the indigo plant, and red obtained from the cochineal insect. Both of these dyestuffs were popular and exported during colonial times. Old garments indicate the use of cochineal on silk and indigo on cotton, as well as the use of other unknown dyes from which yellow and orange tones were obtained. Despite several attempts to revive the tradition of dyeing wool with natural dyes, only a few of the former procedures are still in use.

LEFT: An indigo-dyed shawl displays intricately detailed jaspe motifs.

Jaspe or Ikat

The production of jaspe threads continues to thrive in the western part of the country. These threads are characterized by the figures that emerge when they are woven. Jaspe or ikat is a resist tie-dye technique that consists in tying off specific segments of a skein of thread. When the skein is immersed in the dye bath, only the exposed sections will be colored but not the threads inside the knots. When the ties are removed, the skein has both dyed and undyed segments.

During the weaving process, motifs appear along the length (warp) or width (weft) of the cloth, or in both directions. Traditionally these threads were dyed with natural indigo; later on, when chemical dyes were introduced, dyers added leaves to ferment the dye and obtain a deeper blue. This custom has been lost, and today threads are colored following the manufacturer's directions. The colors most often used for jaspe threads were blue and black and white.

Today, a wide variety of colors and color combinations are found in jaspe. The ingenuity and artistic talent of Maya master dyers has succeeded in giving this cloth a unique character that distinguishes it from ikat produced in other parts of the world.

Guatemala's textiles are so distinctive and valued around the world because of their complex, detailed jaspe patterns (lettering reads "thought"). The perfection that weavers can achieve is extraordinary!

The Loom

The backstrap loom, or "stick-loom," is the connecting thread by which weaving techniques have been passed on for generations. Although its origins are pre-Hispanic, it continues to be very much in use today, primarily by women for weaving their own clothing. The vertical threads (warp) are assembled and the loom is hung; tension is achieved by the use of two straps, one of which is attached to a fixed point (e.g. a tree trunk or pillar), while the other strap goes around the weaver's back at waist level. Next the sticks are set into place, according to the weaver's own techniques and customs. The loom's inherent flexibility made possible the development of many different brocade techniques in which figures emerge as the cloth is woven. Weaving techniques, color and designs are a few of the characteristics that identify the clothing distinctive to each municipality where traditional-style clothing is still worn.

ABOVE: Woman from Chajul, weaving on a backstrap loom. *Photo by Ann Girard courtesy of The Textile Museum of Indigenous Dress, Guatemala.*

ABOVE: Women are now stepping (pun intended) into what has been traditionally a man's world — weaving on a treadle loom. Due to a much-needed income increase, women are beginning to prefer the faster and more efficient treadle loom to the backstrap loom. Aldea Patzaj, Comalapa. *Photo by Ann Girard, 2003, courtesy of The Textile Museum of Indigenous Dress, Guatemala.*

The treadle loom and its necessary implements were introduced to Guatemala during the colonial period when artisans specializing in cloth production arrived from Spain to satisfy the needs of the criollos (creoles), descendants of Spanish settlers. Indigenous men produced wool cloth that they then adopted for certain garments, as well as cotton cloth for women's skirts. Today, the use of the treadle loom has increased considerably, and many textile centers use it to produce large amounts of commercial cloth.

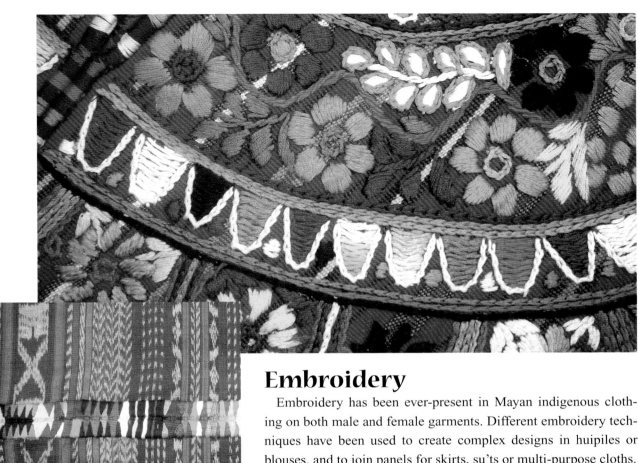

Embroidery

Embroidery has been ever-present in Mayan indigenous clothing on both male and female garments. Different embroidery techniques have been used to create complex designs in huipiles or blouses, and to join panels for skirts, su'ts or multi-purpose cloths.

LEFT AND ABOVE: Two exquisite examples of hand embroidery. The embroidery on the left called "randa," is used to join panels of cloth together. The photo above shows detail of the collar of the huipil from Sumpango, Sacatepéquez.

Sewing machines were introduced in Guatemala at the beginning of the twentieth century. Men learned how to operate them first, and the machines were mainly used to make men's clothing. Years later, machine embroidery became widespread and replaced many traditional techniques, like brocade. At the market nowadays, one finds an array of masterfully embroidered pieces on commercial fabrics that are replacing those woven on backstrap looms, allowing women many more options for replacing traditional garments.

Two shining examples of machine embroidery from Quetzaltenango. The embroidery on the right has a simpler look, while the other is more sophisticated, but both are precious.

Chapter 3
Incorporating
Ethnic
Textiles

More than ever before, cultural diversity is priceless in today's contemporary fiber arts scene, because quilt makers and fiber artists are thirsty for innovation and keen to experiment. The textiles you can acquire nowadays from all over the world bring a never-ending assortment of creative possibilities to your door.

Everyone loves ethnic textiles! Their integral beauty, exotic nature and hand-made qualities are perfect for the quilt-maker's basic, universal principle: We LOVE FABRIC! The more precious, different and unique, the better!

Back in 1999 when I started showing my work in the United States, many people admired my idea of incorporating authentic Guatemalan fabrics into art quilts, and I realized they were craving for rich, unusual ethnic fabrics. They would say, "I didn't know you could use those kinds of textiles in quilts!"; "I have a stash of Japanese silks (or African hand-dyes, or Hungarian indigos) I brought from Tokyo (or Ghana, or Budapest) years ago, but haven't had a clue what to do with them!"; or "I never thought that thicker hand-wovens would work so well and look so good!"

LEFT: Guatemalan hand-woven textiles of all kinds, new and old, in different qualities, being sold at the market. *Photo, Jeff Labanz.*
BELOW LEFT: I made this "free-form" log cabin block with a scrap of brocaded huipil in the center and several different yardage fabrics from around the world. Detail from "Multicolored Sash" (see entire quilt on page 125).
BELOW RIGHT: Detail of block in progress for a future "Multicolored Sash II."

Using native Mayan hand-woven textiles was a natural step in my development as a quilt artist. I was elated, using everything I could put my hands on: hand-woven yardage, found scraps of Mayan blouses (huipiles) and costumes, hand-embroidered decorations (randas) and skirts (cortes). By using the native fabrics, I honor generations of anonymous artists and artisans who came before me and left behind such rich legacies.

Creative Genius

Working with ethnic textiles is both liberating and humbling; it keeps us grounded. We may think we're advanced, inventing new patterns, creating innovative techniques, and then we realize that ancient cultures were already doing the same things centuries ago! Ohio stars are featured on a pre-Columbian ceremonial cape from Peru, and the funeral cloth of a 4,000-year-old Egyptian mummy displays log cabin blocks. It is remarkable that the history of humanity can be told through textiles!

ABOVE LEFT: The "Tree of Life" is a universal symbol that can be seen in textiles from around the world. Amazingly, the meaning is universal as well, usually referring to the fruits of life, the life force or women giving birth.
ABOVE RIGHT: Hand-woven men's pants from Santiago Atitlán, Sololá, display colorful, eight-pointed stars that look very much like an "Ohio Star" quilt block.

Incorporating Ethnic Textiles In Quilts and Wearables

When working with ethnic fabrics, appreciate their unique qualities and respect their distinctive nature. Over the past eight years, I've discovered successful techniques and the most suitable ways of incorporating these precious fabrics in quilts and wearables. Let me share them with you.

Learning about Ethnic Costumes and Textiles

There's a virtual treasure trove of inspiration and enjoyment waiting for you. Check out books on ethnic designs and patterns, including African beadwork and masks, Middle Eastern carpets, American Indian blankets and pottery, Mayan Guatemalan costumes and textiles, Arabic tiles and mosaics or whatever inspires you. Look for multi-cultural traditions in other arts and crafts. See "Recommended Bibliography" on page 138.

Uniqueness

Ethnic textiles have inherent value; they come in infinite forms and suggest endless design possibilities. They are the result of thousands of years of art and craft, passed on through generations by oral tradition. Most of the processes used to make them are labor-intensive, low-tech and time-consuming. These textiles are precious for their unique beauty, and for proudly expressing both the culture and the individual artisan. They are also powerful. Many primitive societies' hunting cloths, initiation shirts, wedding veils, ceremonial and religious clothes were painstakingly made and embellished by hand. It's a common belief that the focus and effort required to produce cloth directs the life force and bestows the textile with special power, an energy all its own.

In the old days, huipiles had a wide, distinctive band woven across the chest. This was called "c'ux" and symbolized the heart, the spiritual center of the garment. A few towns still carry on this custom.

Let's Enjoy the View!

I want to inspire and encourage you to create original quilts and wearables of your own invention. In my experience through teaching quilt making around the world, most people are much more talented and artistic than they give themselves credit for. With this book, I want to empower you to trust and nurture your creative instincts! I want you to begin a fascinating artistic journey, to adventure in new directions and take on exciting fresh projects, to try out different ideas and ways of doing things, to take risks and challenge yourself to jump out of the box (c'mon, it's only fabric). If you accept the challenge, you will grow intuitively, artistically and spiritually as I have. There are no limitations to what you can achieve; only the ones you impose on yourself.

As you read along you will be incorporating different tips and techniques to your "Designer's Toolbox." The goal of this book is not so you can replicate my work exactly. Instead, it is to provide you with a repertoire of design and technical resources that will liberate you to do your craft, and that will make you versatile and flexible enough to tackle any project your heart desires. Later on, this repertoire will become the "ace under your sleeve" to find an unusual solution to a construction problem, or discover the key factor to settle a design dilemma.

This is how I see it. Technique is like when you are learning to drive; you concentrate so much on changing gears, stepping on the brake or gas pedal, and using the mirrors that you cannot enjoy the view.

Having a repertoire of design and technical resources lets you enjoy the view! Your workmanship will continually improve as you practice. Once you have won the wings you'll need to fly "solo," you will be able to concentrate on design and composition rather than agonizing over how things are done. In my opinion, this is a prerequisite to producing superb artwork.

The range of materials (both vegetable and animal in origin) used to make ethnic cloth is infinite, as are the processes and techniques involved. Since hand work is almost always present, slight irregularities are intrinsic to their nature. These irregularities add character and enhance their unique beauty.

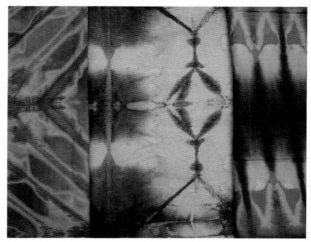

Hand-dyed African fabrics to die for!

Listen to the Fabric

Let it take you by the hand and lead the way. Ethnic cloth has character because of its multi-cultural diversity, and adds individuality to your designs. It has a history and stories to tell. The more I work with ethnic textiles from around the world, the more I want to know about their origins and the motivations behind the fabrics. Where are they from? How are they made? What role do they play in people's lives, and how are they used? What symbols do they include, and what do they mean?

When I started using Guatemalan textiles in my art quilts, I experienced how they took charge almost immediately. My way of working had to adapt to the characteristics of the native cloth. It took me places I would have never gone on my own. So, listen to the fabric and let it take you on an incredible, empowering creative journey!

The Textiles' Noticeable Characteristics

Work only with fabrics you really like. Respond to them emotionally as well as practically. Observe the fabric. How does it make you feel? What characteristics stand out (color, pattern, texture)? How can you use these elements to the best advantage in your design? How will you make this characteristic work for you? Here are two examples of what I mean:

Many of the Guatemalan fabrics are multi-colored. This bothered me at first when I wanted "pure" blue fabrics, for example. Through constant experimentation I realized that instead of cutting out this magenta portion within the blue or fighting against it, I would use it as an "excuse" to expand my color scheme to include blue-violet, violet and red-violet. My quilts are richer now, thanks to this attribute within the hand-woven fabric.

"A Square is A Square..," 2002, 57½" x 60"

Enrich the color blue with a spectrum that goes all the way from blue-green (on the yellow side of the color wheel) to red-violet (on the red side). Neighboring colors enhance each other!

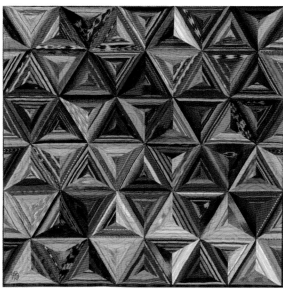

"Aguacatán," 2005, 36" x 37"

Due to the weaving techniques used to make Guatemalan fabrics, many have stripes. I have always loved stripes and saw this characteristic as a great creative opportunity! I set myself a challenge; I would expand the possibilities of stripes as far as they would go! So, I began trying out different ways of cutting patches, with stripes going in every which way. I especially enjoy discovering the surprising sub-patterns that emerge along the seamlines.

Inspiration File

To enhance your creativity, I find it is essential to keep an on-going "Inspiration file." This is a collection of magazine and catalog clippings, photographs, sketches, drawings, fabric scraps, reminder notes to you, which contain ideas of motifs, patterns, compositions, color schemes, etc, that appeal to you.

I keep my own collection as organized as possible in a file cabinet. Items are classified into categories such as "geometrics," "round shapes," "Guatemalan," "masks," "architecture," "improvisational," "color schemes," "African," etc. Inspiration does not usually come out of the blue; it needs something to spark it. When you feel down or out of ideas search the file for something to inspire and motivate you. This file will do the trick every time!

Start a collection in a box, drawer or scrapbook. Begin by gathering up anything that attracts you — subjects or themes, landscapes, patterns, colors, motifs, textures, symbols — from magazines, catalogs, brochures, flyers, napkins, anything! I always have paper and pencil with me to record whatever calls my attention. It may be the motif on a man's shirt, the brick pattern on a wall or the colors in a basket. I keep a camera with me at all times when I am travelling and do not have time to sketch right away. Do not let those glimpses of ideas escape!

When you have a fair amount of clippings, spread them out and absorb the whole. Do you favor geometric forms or organic natural shapes? Is there excitement or boredom? Do you favor light or dark values? Is there variety or are there subjects or colors that are repeated over and over? After this preliminary analysis, classify them into categories. You do not need to know these categories before hand; the clippings will tell you.

This exercise enriches your creative spirit. You will be amazed at what you discover about yourself, your likes and dislikes, your longings and dreams, your tastes and preferences. I am willing to bet that you will also realize that you have more going for yourself than you ever thought!

Use Ethnic Textiles as the Starting Point

Use what's already there! When I use scraps of Mayan blouses, I am always aware that the textile already has a lot going on in terms of color, pattern, texture, symbolism, embellishment and visual richness. Since my goal is to showcase it, instead of adding even more new elements, I expand on it. I choose coordinating colors, shapes and values that will tie the elements of the design together. Choose "blender" fabrics that enhance and complement your main fabrics, not compete with them. Your ethnic fabrics should be the main focus; the blenders are there for support, not to steal the show!

In terms of design, the principle is the same as above; don't add many more visual elements to what is already there. Design is visual order, and your goal is to make the ethnic fabrics stand out and look fantastic. The best way to achieve this is by choosing rather simple designs. Uncomplicated, elegant lines will do the trick every time! Don't use complex, busy compositions that would detract from the fabrics.

The central "huipil" scrap looked best with yellow and purple neighboring blocks. To tie the elements of a design together, reiterate colors taken from the ethnic textiles. Close-up of "We Complement Each Other" (see entire quilt on page 118).

Do Not Seek Perfection!

Perfection is not the point here; motifs don't need to be centered, stripes don't have to match, patches can be dissimilar, and points can be blunt. Give yourself permission to be human; make do, use scraps and cut free-form. Keep in mind that you are dealing with hand-made fabrics that may have irregularities from the maker; your art quilts are allowed to share the same distinctive qualities as the cloth you're using.

Make-do, add another piece if it's too short or cut off excess if it's too long. Motifs need not be centered, strips can be crooked and blocks can be irregular — perfection is not the point! So relax and enjoy the process.

Keep the Integrity of the Cloth

Use large pieces to show off the natural beauty of the cloth. There's no point in cutting exquisite, hand-made textiles into small pieces; show them off in big chunks instead!

The smallest-size patch I cut is 3½" (3" finished). The smallest-size "traditional" block I usually make is about 5" or 6" (finished).

The central kaleidoscope uses mainly commercial fabrics in pieces that may be as small as one-half inch. Notice the contrast in the use of ethnic fabrics on the inner and outer borders; they were cut in extra-large chunks to preserve the integrity of the cloth and show its inherent natural beauty! Detail "Chichi's Cross," 2003, 47" x 47" (see entire quilt on page 130).

Some people worry that using another culture's materials in their artwork may be in some way disrespectful. I had a solo show at the National Museum of Modern Art in Guatemala City in May 2002. The Minister of Culture at the time, Otilia Lux de Cotí, was a native Mayan who always wore her ethnic group's attire proudly. Her opening address put my mind at ease:

"Priscilla's work relates to our culture and brings to life what I refer to as positive inter-culturality. Through her artistic and symbolic work, she shows us that the distinctive Guatemalan ethnicities can coexist in harmony, respecting each other's identity.

What is most important, from my point of view, is that being a novel proposal [the art quilts], the artist doesn't damage or attack in any way this cultural expression [the Mayan textile] but maintains its authenticity. In this way, the artist confirms that creativity can be intercultural, as long as you value the sources of inspiration and treat them with respect."

Panoramic view of my solo show at the National Museum of Modern Art, Guatemala, May 2002. A real paper and bamboo kite hanging from the ceiling added realism to my renderings of kites.

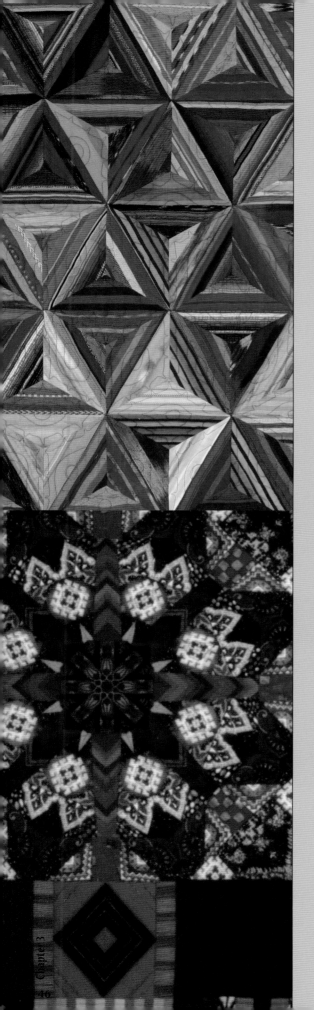

Motivating and Challenging Quilt-making

- Make it a point of stretching the envelope continually. Keep an open mind; do not reject that new idea so quickly — give your brain a chance to accommodate! Make some far-out decisions (even if they may be timid for someone else, they are "far out" for you, and that is all that matters).

- Try to learn something new with every quilt you make, be it a technique/new product or material/gadget/style. This is stimulating and will keep you interested; pretty soon you will be hooked on innovation! Few things are so boring and discouraging as staying within your comfort level for too long. When you can do it "with your eyes closed," it is time to move on!

- Learn about other art forms and crafts outside quilting. They will give you tons of ideas and inspiration:
  - Painting teaches you about color, value, texture, composition.
  - Mosaics are very similar to quilts in that they are done with pieces; tile floors are a great source of inspiration for repetitive grid designs and borders.
  - Beading and jewelry-making teach you to be precise and pay close attention to details.
  - Knitting and crochet teach you about patterns and textures.
  - Paper collage teaches you to work in a spontaneous, improvisational way. This engages your right-brain which enables you to work more intuitively (instead of rationalizing everything to death). It is an excellent training to free yourself from conventionalisms.
  - Fabric dyeing teaches you about color and color mixing in surprising ways!
  - Scrapbooking teaches you organization and balance.

- Variety is a great resource! Use it as often as possible.
- You don't have to use the same technique throughout your quilt ... you can piece the background, appliqué the leaves, crazy quilt the border ...
- Vary the color scheme from one project to the next. To add visual interest and energy within a quilt, vary the values, fabric scale, patterns, and textures. Why use four fabrics when you can use forty?

  The exhilaration of being motivated, of loving what you do, and of being passionate about your projects is one of the best feelings in the world!

Mixing and Matching your Fabric Palette

You will probably want to use an assortment or mix of ethnic fabrics in each quilt. Using only one kind would be too busy, too overwhelming or just plain boring! Try staying within one same style or "look." I would not advise adding sophisticated motifs (e.g. Jacobean or art nouveau) unless that is exactly the look you are after. Combining very different style motifs can be tricky.

Guatemalan textiles (G's) are the main component in my work, but I team them up with other fabrics that share the same rustic, primitive, hand-made qualities for visual interest, added richness and variety of pattern, scale, color, value and texture.

This is my stash of Guatemalan textiles and my collection of belts and sashes. *Photo, Pamela Cerezo.*

An example of the "fabric mix" that I use in my quilts.

My first fabric collection for Robert Kaufman, based on Guatemalan textiles, premiered in fall 2004.

Through constant experimentation, I have come to realize that I can incorporate other exciting fabrics that are in sync with the spirit of the G's. Commercial cottons (plaids, stripes, geometrics, homespun, ethnic-looking and hand-made-looking prints), other ethnics (African prints and mudcloth, Indonesian batiks, Australian aboriginal, Japanese yukatas, South African indigos, wax Java Dutch prints), and hand-dyed, hand-painted fabrics, among others, mix well with the G's to create rich, varied quilts. This exotic fabric mixing and matching creates a well-balanced, eye-pleasing design with a rich contemporary look and lots of character! See "Resources" on page 140 for a listing of stores that carry ethnic fabrics.

It is amazing to realize the diversity of fabric types that can go into a quilt. There are some fabrics you simply cannot imagine putting together, but they look amazing together! A visitor to one of my local shows asked how I thought to use some "hideous" fabrics (yep! that's the word he used) and make them look good together.

One of the qualities I love most about making quilts is the almost magical way in which zillions of fabric pieces of all sorts come together and become one when you sew them into a "wholecloth." Suddenly, everything makes sense. All those hours agonizing over which shade was better than which seem pointless. The quilt has become one with you and with itself.

I have prepared three luscious layouts: a warm color range, a cool color range and an assortment of earth tones. I am sure that some choices will amaze you. Now you can mix and match your own unique combinations with everyday commercial textiles. At last, you can start creating with fabrics that seemed too precious to cut up. Drool away!

Advantages of Using Commercial Cottons

1. Commercial cottons and other fabrics will help define your style and your design.

2. Since ethnic fabrics are often heavier, mixing them with commercial cottons will help avoid bulky seams.

3. Commercial cottons are more stable, so they won't let the looser weave be distorted; they will hold it in place and serve as a guide for size and shape.

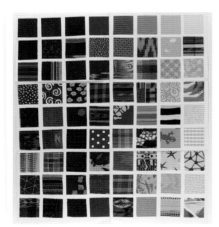

Warm tones.

Cool tones.

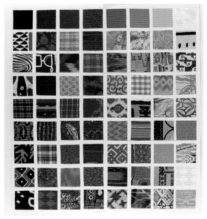

Earth tones.

Fabric Preparation

Pre-Washing or Not?

I strongly recommend that you pre-wash all Guatemalan textiles prior to using, because they do shrink and release excess dye that tints the water in the washing machine. I always pre-wash them, to be on the safe side, even for a wall hanging that will not be washed. To do so, follow instructions below. Follow manufacturer's directions to pre-wash other ethnic fabrics as well, if desired.

You may choose to pre-wash commercial fabrics or not. I buy good quality fabrics, and I usually do not pre-wash them for a wall hanging, but I do pre-wash them for a bed quilt.

Before Washing:

- Zigzag or serge edges to prevent excessive fraying (optional).
- Separate fabrics into darks and lights by color. Be especially careful with blues and reds, as they tend to bleed.
- Using a gentle cycle, machine wash with hot/wash temperature and warm/rinse.
- Add 1 teaspoon of Retayne per yard of fabric to the wash water. This fixative will ensure that colors stay bright and do not run. You can purchase Retayne at any quilt shop or buy it online.
- Do not worry if the water in the machine is dark colored. This is the excess dye being released and will not stain your fabrics.
- Remove fabrics immediately after the wash cycle is finished. Leaving them crumpled and damp could stain them.
- Tumble dry at coolest temperature for about half an hour. Remove fabrics promptly and hang them to complete the drying process.
- Ironing is optional.

Shrinkage

Due to its handmade nature, the fabric does shrink an average of 6% (1"-2" per yard) after washing. Take this into account when calculating yardage for a project.

Qualities and Care Instructions

Guatemalan hand-woven textiles (G's) are wholesome and stable; however, people often have misconceptions. When you mention G's, they tend to think of a thick, dull, almost upholstery-weight fabric that would not be suitable for quilting. There are many different varieties and weights of G's — from gauze to upholstery to thick tapestry — as well as different qualities. The kind that I use for quilting is soft, lightweight and made of 100% mercerized cotton, which gives it a nice silk-like sheen.

I like its body, its feel, its weight. It is sturdy and holds its shape when ironed. On the other hand, the looser weave makes it very fudgeable, which is always convenient. G's don't ravel with normal handling and are durable.

But one of the best qualities is the fact that they are reversible! This is a wonderful feature when working with symmetry, or when you forgot to turn over your template for cutting reverse pieces by mistake! No problemo — just flip the patch over, and ta-da!

Width

Fabric is 34" to 35" wide, a rare collector's item found only in fabrics made before the 1930s. This is when the industry's standard began to change to the 44" width we are so familiar with today.

Fading

Just like any other 100% cotton fabric, Guatemalan textiles may fade over time, so keep them away from direct sunlight.

Fabric Aids

Although Guatemalan fabrics are a bit thicker and more loosely woven than commercial cottons, there is no need to use a stabilizer. They are stable and sturdy, and they don't ravel.

I don't use spray starch or sizing either, because I like the soft hand of the pre-washed fabric. I find its stretchiness and fudge ability very convenient.

Quality and Precision

People often ask how I make my quilts so precise. Quality and precision do not just happen, they are something you have to build into every step of the design process and quilt construction. Here are some tips.

1. Buy materials of the best quality you can afford. Your time and effort invested in the project will be the same with either good quality or cheap materials.

2. Techniques can also add value to your work or be poor and diminish it. Workmanship has to be at the service of design; practice, practice, practice and experiment with new ways to perfect your workmanship. If, for example, your design calls for perfectly matching stripes or a straight line, and some match and some do not or the line is crooked, your quilt will look sloppy. This will distract the viewer and spoil the integrity of the design. Good-quality materials and techniques will make a big difference in the look and permanence of your quilt or wearable. Quality is of the utmost importance, and pays off through years of enjoyment.

3. Set aside some quiet time without interruptions so you can focus.

4. Measure exactly.

5. Make templates with care and trim points for a perfect match (detailed instructions on page 56 "Making Templates").

6. Cutting mistakes will not take care of themselves, so cut all your pieces accurately.

7. Sew pieces and blocks together aligning all sides, not only the one you're sewing on at the moment; this simple tip will increase your precision incredibly!

8. Do not finger press, it isn't nearly adequate for ethnic fabrics. Use lots of steam instead! Press, applying pressure on the wrong side, after stitching every single seam. Flip over and iron from side to side on the right side.

9. Press seams open whenever two ethnic fabrics are sewn together and always when joining rows! If for some reason seams are too bulky, Paula Nadelstern taught me that you can always press them to submission!

10. Square-off finished blocks or units, if necessary, before putting rows together. Hand-woven fabrics especially may tend to stretch out of place. Squaring them off will keep them to exact size, but do not overdo it ... trim as little as possible.

11. For borders, measure quilt through the center on both directions.

12. To prepare the quilt sandwich, pull all layers gently on all sides, to square it as best as possible.

13. After it has been quilted, square using a carpenter's metal set square (for corners) and long, metal ruler for sides.

14. Apply my "all-by-machine" binding (instructions on page 63).

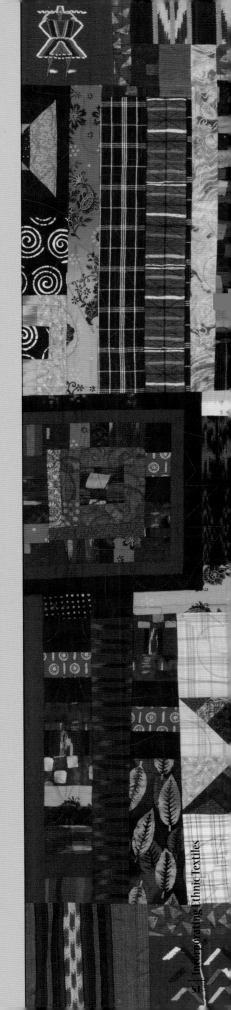

Chapter 4

Getting Started

Essential Tools and Materials

You will need all the basic quilting supplies and notions, including:

- Rotary cutter and cutting mat
- Rulers — My favorite are Quilter's Rule, because they have built-in grip and will not slip. They also have basic markings that won't confuse you. The four essential rulers are:
  - 6½" square
  - 12½" square
  - 14" x 4½" rectangular
  - 24" x 6½" rectangular
- 1⅜" super-fine glass head silk pins for piecing and general sewing
- Large 2" flower–head pins for sandwiching quilts
- Sewing machine with specialized presser feet
- ¼" Little Foot, or quarter–inch patchwork foot
- Walking foot for quilting straight lines
- Big Foot, or darning foot for free-form quilting
- General purpose foot for machine appliqué (zigzag, satin stitch and/or blind stitch) and for sewing in general
- Hand and sewing machine needles

- Neutral, medium gray or beige cotton thread for piecing (both upper and bobbin thread)
- Matching color thread for binding
- Matching polyester thread for garments
- Monofilament thread (clear or smoke) for invisible appliqué
- Rayon embroidery threads for decorative satin stitching and/or quilting
- Bobbins
- Seam ripper (indispensable!)
- Measuring tape
- Fabric scissors
- Paper/template scissors
- Plastic template material (sheets with an ⅛" grid and bold inch lines)
- A thin, clear plastic ruler (with an ⅛" grid and bold inch lines)
- Permanent ultra–fine marker (for templates)
- Adhesive sandpaper dots or cushiony, clear plastic dots like Fabric Grabbers or 3M
- Iron and ironing board

Cutting

Getting pieces to match easily and accurately comes from good cutting. If you cut something correctly from the start, your pieces will match effortlessly. So paying attention when cutting pays off! The projects in this book use templates because they yield accurate results every time. I make many of my art quilts this way because I like precision, and your project will be more enjoyable when all of the pieces fit together like they are supposed to. Do not worry; I have included time-saving cutting techniques whenever possible to speed up the process.

A cutting mat is mandatory when using a rotary cutter. Use the largest mat your space allows. I have an extra-large mat that covers the entire surface of my studio table. It's practical and comfortable, because I do not have to keep checking how far I am cutting or worry that I will run out of mat space and damage the table or the blade.

Use sharp blades and change them quite often. Going over pins dulls and nicks the blades, so beware.

My cutting/designing/assembling table with its cutting mat. My design wall (at right) is narrow, so when the door to my son's bathroom is closed, it becomes part of the design wall. When I am working on a big project, the bathroom door will be banned for days! *Photo, Pamela Cerezo.*

Masking Tape

I could not live without masking tape! I use it for all kinds of things, especially for keeping track of the order in which patches go as I am constructing the quilt. I number the beginning of rows, vertically or horizontally as needed.

I will number every single patch if the design is complex, or if it has taken me weeks to decide where everything goes and I do not want to risk losing the exact placement. I also use it to make marks. For example, when I am chain piecing, I put a small piece of masking tape to all "left" side patches so I don't get confused. Using tape is faster, cleaner and more visible than other marking methods like pinning or using chalk. Test different brands of masking tape; some will get "gunky" if left on for months, and others will get gooey if ironed. Use a permanent marker that won't run or stain to write on it.

Cut Several Layers at Once

Cutting two or more layers of fabric at a time can speed things up. Begin with two layers and add one more at a time as you acquire confidence and skill. Commercial fabrics may be stacked up to four layers; ethnic fabrics up to two. This is not worth doing if the cut pieces are not accurate, so focus and cut cautiously.

Always cut a few extra blocks or units. I make anywhere from three to six extra blocks (e.g. Log Cabin blocks) or cut up to 10 to 25 extra patches (e.g. "Flora" tumbler patches), because there are always some blocks that look better than others. Making more than I need gives me the flexibility of choosing the very best units and discarding the no-it-doesn't-belong-in-this-quilt ones. This will tremendously improve the visual quality of your work!

Incorporate extra blocks into the backing, make a conversation-piece label, or collect odd blocks and practice special settings.

Assortment of "extra" blocks from previous projects; they somehow found their way into new quilts.

Making Templates

Making exact templates is essential to accurate piecing and true measurements. Use an ultra-fine permanent marker, a thin, clear plastic ruler with ⅛" grid and bold inch lines, and plastic template material. I prefer a ⅛" grid with bold inch lines because the visual reference is very helpful. Use clear if you wish.

All of the templates in this book include seam allowances unless otherwise noted. With masking tape, secure the plastic material over the outline of the template so it will not slip. Trace the outline precisely and cut carefully.

You'll notice that many templates in this book have trimmed/snipped points. This is an essential factor for accurate piecing alignment. I strongly recommend you get into the habit of doing this. Line up neighboring templates right-sides together as if you were going to sew them, matching sewing lines. You'll see "dog's ears" extending beyond; trim off this excess. Later on, make this extra little cut. It will make your patches match perfectly and improve your workmanship!

For the final step, adhere sandpaper or cushiony clear plastic dots to the underside of the templates. This helps in several ways. It makes it easier on your wrists by preventing slippage so you don't have to hold the template so tight, and it also prevents shaving the template; by elevating it just a tad, it provides an edge for the rotary cutter's blade to go along instead of going over it.

A Sewing Space of Your Own

The only way to go if you are serious about devoting time to the art of making quilts is with a creative space of your own. This will send everyone (beginning with yourself) the right message — that this is for real, that it is a priority, and that you are planning on doing it for extended periods of time.

You will not go far if whenever you want to work on a project you first have to bring every single little thing out to e.g. the dining room table, and then have to put it all away just 'cause the family wants to eat dinner (shoot!). Few things are more discouraging than these lengthy, complicated preparations. Everyone else's time and activities cut into your creative space. This situation is frustrating, impractical and inefficient.

Okay, so we agree you need a creative space of your own. Some people are lucky enough to have a whole room dedicated to their quilt making, but do not be deterred if you don't. Think creatively to find a suitable space; it can be any underutilized area within your home (any of the kids moving out soon?). It can be a large table in a corner, a closet's cubby hole, or half of a bedroom. What is important is to have a haven for creative productivity that is always ready when you feel like working.

The goal is to have a creative haven of your own where:

- You can organize and store all necessary equipment and supplies within easy reach;

- You can leave ongoing projects midway knowing they will be undisturbed and out of everyone's way;

- You can be free to do as you please, no explanations required.

Keep in mind:

- Good lighting is a must! Analyze the time frames during which you will be sewing to determine the best lighting required.

- Storage space is at a premium! Build in as much as possible and complement it with stackable containers in different shapes and sizes.

- Isolate yourself and set aside long periods of time to work in your refuge, especially in the beginning creative stages of a project. ("Creative genius at work, do not disturb.")

Acrylic (Ready-Made) Templates

Shops offer a wide variety of ready-made acrylic templates. I have them in all shapes and sizes and love working with them. They are thick (at least ⅛"), providing a comfortable, safe edge for the rotary cutter. They are easier to hold (adhere sandpaper or clear plastic dots to these too), and easier and faster to use.

You can even make your own — bring an accurate outline of the shape/size you want to a shop that makes acrylic signs.

Using Templates

Most projects provide time-saving techniques for speedier cutting. First, you'll cut a specific size strip of fabric, and then you will cut patches from this strip using a template. Don't trace the template on the fabric, because it is time-consuming and will not show on some thicker fabrics. Instead, align the ruler with the template's edge and cut; or, if you have experience and are extremely careful, simply run the rotary cutter along the template's edge. This may be dangerous because the blade is extremely sharp, so do not try it if you are not skilled with the rotary cutter. Cut during the day, when there is good lighting and you are well-rested and focused. To prevent accidents, change to a different task when tired.

Sewing Different Types of Fabrics

My tips on sewing are simple. Know your sewing machine; refer to the instruction booklet often. Clean it periodically to keep it lint-free and in good working order. Use the appropriate needle for the job at hand, and change it often.

Use ¼" seams for piecing all the projects in this book, unless indicated otherwise. Use the appropriate presser foot for each task, and chain stitch whenever possible (see detailed explanation on page 59).

Sewing together different types of fabrics with unusual weaves and varying weights is perfectly okay! You'll be surprised to see how many precious fabrics you never thought of as "candidates" for quilting are not only suitable, but they work and look great!

Tip

When sewing together one commercial fabric with one thicker ethnic fabric, put the thicker, looser woven fabric underneath and let your machine's feed dogs take care of the looser weave for you.

Pressing Unique Fabrics

When pressing, always take into account the weight of the fabric. When in doubt, follow the fabric's lead. Flip it over on your ironing board, and press in the natural direction the fabric tends to go.

• Use lots of steam! It makes these fabrics lie as flat as a pancake!

• When sewing with ethnic fabrics, your only concern should be avoiding bulky seams.

• When sewing together one commercial fabric and one thicker ethnic fabric, always iron toward the lighter weight fabric and away from the heavier ethnic fabrics. In other words, the thicker, heavier fabric rules!

• When sewing together two thicker ethnic fabrics, press seams open.

Back of an unquilted, pieced top.

Direction of Seams

When constructing a quilt in the traditional way, press seams that will be joined together in opposite directions. This ensures that the seams will align, and it helps distribute the bulk to create a nice, flat quilt.

Ruth McDowell taught me not to worry about clipping seams; a quilt will be secured by the quilting, and besides, it does not suffer the stress that a garment does. Flip the lightest weight fabric to the opposite side; match seams, pin and stitch entire seam. After stitching, go back and clip; press as is.

Borders

For border strips, be sure to measure top-to-bottom and left-to-right along the center of the quilt to ensure accuracy.

Mitered Borders

1. Calculate the length of the border strips for mitered corners like this:
Width of the quilt + width of the border + at least 5" to 6" extra for mitering
(more if border is over 4" wide).

2. Center the border and stitch, beginning and ending ¼" away from the corner's edge.

3. Bring the quilt to the ironing board. Lay the corner perfectly flat, and iron it out with your hands. Straighten both border strips (one goes underneath, and the other crosses over on top). Take the top one, and fold to the inside at a 45-degree angle. Use a square ruler with a diagonal line to check square edges and proper alignment. Press gently so the crease stays in place. Carefully, slide the ruler underneath all of the layers so nothing gets disturbed. Pin the fold generously to the underside.

4. Bring to the sewing machine, and either edgestitch with coordinating thread or blind stitch with monofilament thread (which I prefer). You will have perfect mitered borders every time!

Make a Sample Block

I strongly recommend that you make a sample block/unit or two before cutting fabric for the entire quilt. There are many advantages to doing this. When you try out one block, you become familiar with the entire process: You understand details or aspects that were not clear on paper, you can check if everything fits the way it's supposed to, and you can see if the fabric choices and placement are appropriate.

Make sample blocks.

Techniques

Secure Stitching

When sewing different types of fabrics together, especially loosely woven fabrics, it is important to make sure that your seams will not come undone. Secure your stitches at the beginning and end of every seam (every patch, every section) by sewing 1-2 stitches in reverse or in "0" stitch length. Some new machines can be programmed to do this automatically.

Chain Piecing

Chain piecing is an efficient, time-saving method for sewing many patches continuously. Feed two patches right sides together (RST) through the sewing machine, securing stitching at the beginning and the end. Feed the next set of patches RST, and continue sewing without interruption. Do not stop to cut thread tails. When you are done sewing, bring the "chain" to the ironing board. Patches may be ironed as is, or you may prefer to separate them first.

Strip Piecing

This technique refers to creating "new" fabric by piecing together long strips of fabrics lengthwise into a strip set. The strips may or may not vary in width. Patchwork shapes are then cut from this "new" fabric.

This technique is also a great way to use up many different, narrow strips and scraps, and it does not matter if they are straight or not! In fact, you will get wonderful, interesting variations with slanted and crooked strips.

Two of my quilts being done by my quilter extraordinaire and friend, Laura Lee Fritz, at her studio in Alaska! *Photo, Laura Lee Fritz.*

Making the Quilt Sandwich

Prepare the quilt sandwich by laying the backing on the bottom with right side facing out, the batting in the middle and the quilt top on top. Baste using your favorite method. Quilt as you please, or machine quilt with an overall pattern.

I like my pieces to hang straight so I prefer lightweight cotton batting that will not add bulk or puffiness.

Using a Design Wall

In all my classes it is mandatory that students work on an improvised 2-yd. length of flannel design wall. I am usually amazed by the fact that most of the students have never used such an indispensable, vital design aid before. Throughout the class I hear comments like, "What a difference it makes to see my work up on the wall," "How easy it is to move the pieces around as I please ['cause they stick to the flannel] and how much fun it is … it's like playing!" and "The moment I get back home I'll make myself a permanent design wall!" They also wonder how they have lived without it!

The only way a dressmaker can asses if a garment looks good, is by fitting it on the body of the person who will wear it. A flower arrangement that goes on a round foyer table has to be created on a turntable that enables the florist to view it from all sides! And, an art quilt that will hang from the wall has to be created — yep, you guessed it — on a wall! This is the perspective where it will be viewed from!

ADVANTAGES:

1. The freedom and ease of moving your pieces around until you find a pleasing arrangement. Although I have to warn you, this can be too much fun and you can easily get caught in the excitement. A given set of pieces can yield MANY different designs so, in theory, you could continue to play *ad eternum*, but you have to make up your mind eventually. There comes a time when you have to stop playing and start sewing!

2. Working in this way saves you "ripping" time. I have noticed that many students jump ahead and start sewing, without really knowing what it is they will be doing. Afterwards I hear them say "Oh no, I should have put that there!" and go for the frustrating ripper. Take your time; do not start sewing any pieces together until you have figured out the entire design and made ALL of your decisions. Analyze your design and plan the best construction strategy. What to do first, what next, etc. Sewing is usually the easy part.

Finishing Touches

The finishing touches for your work of art are the hanging sleeve, quilt label, a professionally-finished binding and your signature.

Hanging Sleeve Preparation:

1. Cut a piece of fabric that is 2" less than the width of the top of the quilt x 8" wide.

2. Finish both short ends with a narrow hem. (Turn raw edge ¼" and again, another ¼" and sew with a straight stitch.)

3. Fold in half lengthwise and press. Both long raw edges should align.

Sewing Hanging Sleeve to Back of Quilt:

1. Once you are finished quilting, cut away excess batting and backing by squaring off all four edges. For accuracy, I use a carpenter's large metal set square (L-shaped ruler).

2. Center and pin the long raw edges of the folded hanging sleeve along the raw edge of the quilt top on the back. There should be about 1¼" to 1½" of clear space on both ends, which will conceal the rod or slat used to hang the quilt.

3. The use of a digital or Polaroid camera is strongly recommended. When you have come to an arrangement you may not be crazy about, but you like, take a picture before deciding to try something else. That way, if after playing for a while you realize that you really liked the original arrangement after all, you will have a visual reference to go back to. Taking pictures is also a great way to document your creative process step by step. It is also helpful for keeping track of which fabrics go into a quilt (take close-ups to capture as much detail as possible). This will be an excellent reference for future quilts.

4. A reducing glass is a crucial tool that I could not live without. Good substitutes are a peephole or a camera's viewfinder. My studio is rather small, so I cannot physically step away from the wall but a few feet. This gadget lets me give my works in progress a "bird's-eye view." It is the only way in which you can assess DESIGN aspects like:

• **Balance:** Is the overall balance of the piece effective? Does it look heavier in any one area? Does it feel like it is tilted or falling down?

• **Value:** The placement of lights and darks. Are there any patches that stand out like a sore thumb and need deleting or replacing? Any dull areas that need spicing up?

• **Composition:** The overall flow of the work. Is it pleasing? Is it too busy or too plain? Shall I get rid of some elements or add new ones? Is the design exciting and energetic? Or predictable, too repetitive and boring?

• **Contrast:** Are there patches or areas of the quilt that "disappear"? Do I want a soft edge with low or no contrast? Or a hard edge with high contrast? Are the pieces blending too much or not enough?

To make a quick and easy design wall, cover a 1"-thick foam board with neutral colored, solid flannel (ecru, medium gray, beige) and hang in place. Once you start working on it and discovering its many advantages, you too will wonder how have you managed without it.

Binding:

With my "all-by-machine binding method," you will start placing and sewing the binding on the wrong/back side of your quilt. This way, the upper edge of the hanging sleeve will be caught between the quilt and the binding twice. (Once when you first sew the binding from the back; and a second time when you edgestitch the binding from the front of the quilt.) The binding will be attached very securely.

Note: If quilt is larger than 40" square, it is best to make two hanging sleeves — one for the top and one for the bottom. The bottom weight will keep the quilt hanging perfectly straight.

Quilt Label

Preparation:

I like to print my labels at home, using an inkjet printer. I make them 8½" x 5½" (half letter size), because I like to write in as much about the quilt's design, inspiration and general information as possible. Print two labels at a time, and use up the entire sheet.

To print my quilt labels on silk, I buy a kit from Jacquard Products (see "Resources" on page 140), which includes six 8½" x 11" sheets of silk fused to freezer paper, a bottle of fixative and an instruction booklet. I prefer to use silk because it gives the best resolution, even with small lettering. To give the label a more tailored look, I line it with soft, thin muslin.

To continue:

1. Put label and muslin right sides together.

2. With a ¼" seam, sew only three sides (left, top and right sides). The bottom of the label should remain unsewn.

3. Finger press the seams toward the muslin as far into the corners as possible.

4. Snip off corners and gently turn label to the right side.

5. Press lovingly.

Sewing label to quilt:

To sew the label to the quilt, I use the same trick as with the hanging sleeve: I align the raw bottom edges of the lined label to the raw bottom edge of the quilt. Pin all around the label as you straighten it up. I catch the bottom of the label with two rows of seams when I sew the binding on to the quilt (back and front).

Slipstitch the other three sides by hand.

"All-By-Machine" Binding Method

Cutting:

1. Cut binding strips 2½" wide (crosswise) by the full width of the fabric. This way, you will not have to struggle when turning it to finish.

Preparation:

2. Sew strips right sides together at a 45-degree angle to make one long binding strip. Cut off excess, leaving a ¼" allowance.

3. Fold long binding strip in half lengthwise, wrong sides together, and press.

4. Unfold left end of the strip only. Turn left bottom corner and align with upper edge (forming a 45-degree diagonal fold), press. Cut along this crease.

5. Fold raw edge ¼" to the inside, press. Re-fold long binding strip as in Step 3 and press again. (We'll refer to this as a "pocket" later on.)

Process:

6. Please note, you will begin pinning and sewing the binding on the back side of your quilt. This is the most important trick to successfully do an all-by-machine binding.

7. Use a walking foot on your machine. Beginning about 5" inside the "pocket" end of the strip, start sewing a ¼" seam. The end of the long binding strip will be tucked into this "pocket" at the end of the round. So, make sure to keep it free until later.

8. Corners. To achieve a neat-looking binding, special attention needs to be paid to accurately folding and sewing corners. STOP sewing ¼" away from the edge, secure your stitches, and cut the thread.

9. Fold back the binding at a 45-degree angle.

10. Now, fold over the binding on itself. Start sewing again on the other side of the binding, beginning ¼" away from the edge.

11. End of the binding round. Once you have sewn the binding all around the quilt, you are ready to finish it neatly. Cut the binding strip 1" longer than needed, and tuck the raw edge inside the "pocket" you created at the beginning. Secure the opening with a pin, so it will stay put when turning to the front side.

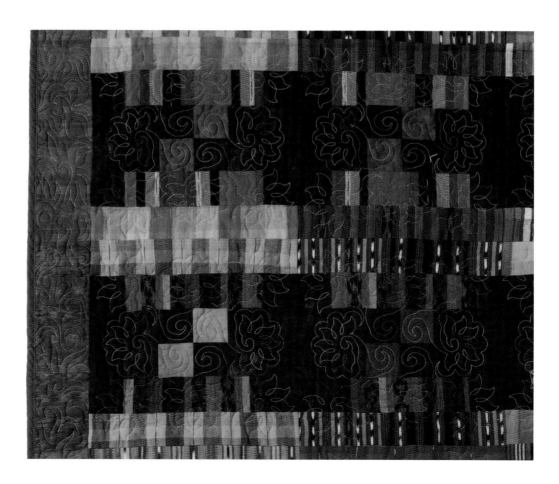

Finishing

Now comes the exciting part! I love to do the binding, for it gives me a sense of accomplishment of a job well done! Turn the quilt over so that the top (front) will be facing you. Bring binding over to the front and edgestitch with care. There is no need to pin, except at the very beginning and at corners. Use your left hand constantly, to smooth out and tuck the quilt inside the binding for a perfect finish.

If you are insecure or anxious about how straight your seam will look, here are a few tips that can help you:

a. Use matching color thread; a tad darker is even better.

b. Use mono-filament thread so your stitches will not show. This is also a good idea when your binding fabric is multi-colored, and you don't want to change threads in mid-stream.

c. Pin a few inches ahead of your seam; remove and re-position pins along the way.

d. Sew only a few inches at a time, stop and check your progress. Do not be overly perfectionist. Nobody will notice a little crooked seam somewhere, and it should not bother you either. (Now, don't you go pointing it out!) Go on, you're doing just fine.

12. Corners: No need to stop at corners now, the front seam is done in one uninterrupted stretch. Bring the needle down 2-3" before the corner and stop. Tug on the binding and fold straight all the way past the corner.

13. Carefully turn over bottom folded binding to the front side; pin. Continue sewing down to the inside corner, bring needle down, pivot, and continue sewing.

14. Secure stitches. Bury thread tails inside batting. And ... *voilá*! You have a professionally finished binding in no time at all!

Signing Your Artwork

You're creating art, so it is more than appropriate that you sign your work. And, since it's made up of thread and cloth, what would be more fitting than to embroider your signature?

Free-form embroider your signature using a narrow zigzag, topstitch needle size #14 and good quality rayon thread. Practice on paper first, internalizing the movements; mark fabric lightly and go over it slowly so it's nice and full.

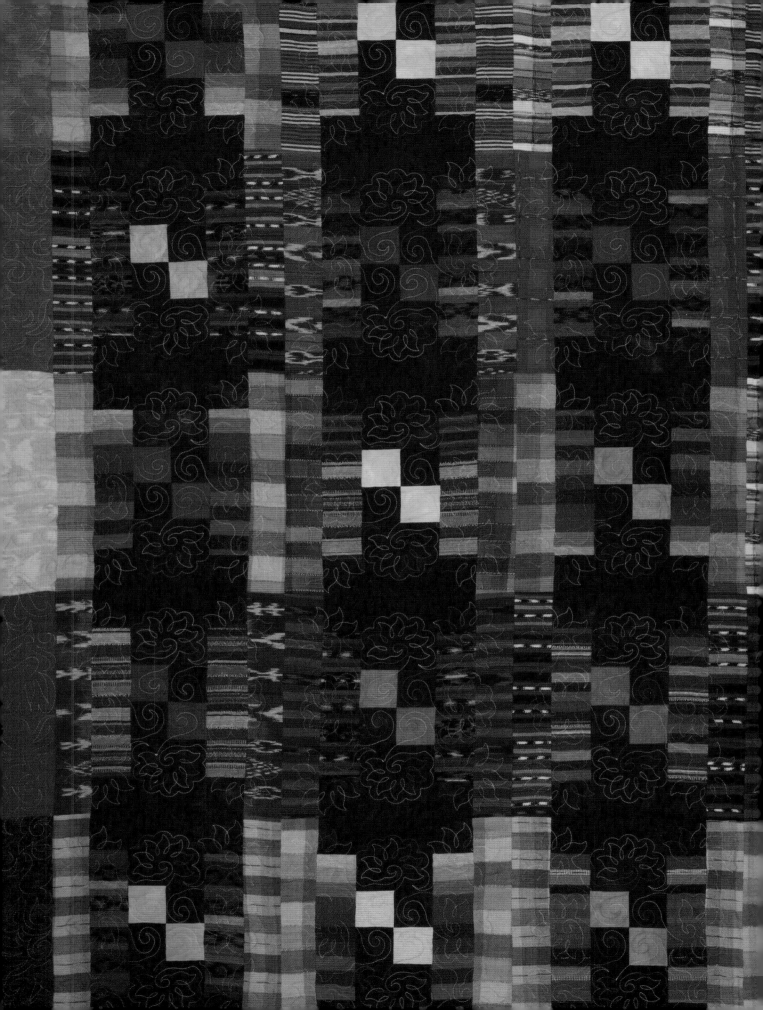

Chapter 5
Projects
from Ethnic
Inspiration

It's a quilt, it's a mat, no it's a sawdust rug! During Holy Week the entire community of Antigua, Guatemala, gathers to create stunning sawdust rugs as a sign of religious faith and reverence. Isn't it just like a quilt though? It even has borders! *Photo, Jeff Labanz.*

Here is a Guatemalan version of a Baltimore Beauty rendered in multicolored sawdust.
Photo, Jeff Labanz.

Quilting imagery is very much alive and present in Guatemala. Everywhere I look, there is a quilt waiting to happen — there are block patterns, border motifs and quilting designs all around us. I will share ten of my favorite projects so you can turn your initial excitement into inspiration and creativity that results in fresh, vibrant and innovative quilts, wall hangings and wearables, with high visual impact and a completely different look.

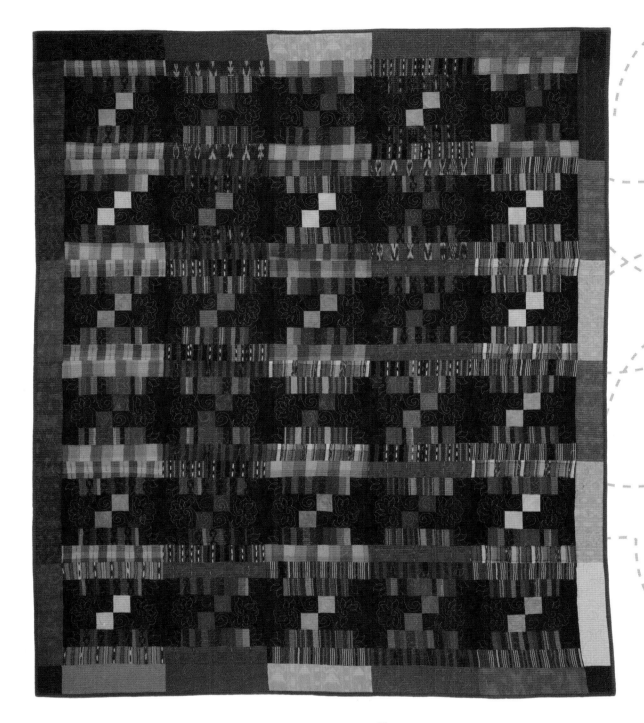

Mayan Rainbow

Finished Quilt: 68" x 80"   Finished Block: 12"   Quilted By: Tina Collins

To make this quilt, I used every single hand-woven fabric in my stash at the time. It was such an explosion of color that I decided to use one dark navy batik throughout the background to keep things under control. I enjoyed whizzing through strips and strips of fabric, and the project went very quickly. As I was making it, the blocks' staggered look suggested to me the steps from ancient Mayan temples, thus the name. The Maya built tall, monumental buildings with hundreds of steps reaching up to the gods.

Fabric and Cutting Directions:

2 YD. BLACK BATIK

- Cut into 26 strips, 2½" wide.

- From 4 of the strips, cut 60 squares 2½" x 2½".

- From 7 of the strips, cut 60 rectangles 2½" x 4½".

- From 15 of the strips, cut 60 rectangles 2½" x 8½".

¼ YD. EACH OF 12 SOLIDS (lime, teal, dark green, turquoise, red, orange, yellow, coral, magenta, navy, medium purple and dark purple).

- From each of the solid fabrics, cut 1 strip 3½" wide. Set aside the 3½"-wide dark purple strip. From the remaining 3½" strips, cut 3 rectangles 3½" x 12½".

- From the 3½" dark purple strip, cut 4 squares 3½" x 3½".

- From each of the solid fabrics, cut 1 strip 2½" wide.

- From each of the strips, cut 6 squares 2½" x 2½" (extra squares allow for block center color manipulation).

½ YD. EACH OF 12 STRIPES AND PLAIDS IN A VARIETY OF COLORS.

- From each stripe and plaid fabric, cut 5 strips 2½" wide.

- From 3 of the strips of each of the stripe and plaid fabrics, cut 9 rectangles 2½" x 12½".

- From 2 of the strips of each of the stripe and plaid fabrics, cut 8 rectangles 2½" x 8½" (extra rectangles allow for color manipulation).

⅝ YD. FABRIC FOR BINDING

- From the binding fabric, cut 8 strips 2¼" wide.

4¼ YD. FABRIC FOR BACKING

Constructing Blocks:

Fabric placement for each block must be determined before sewing the block.
To construct one block:

1. Sew 1 solid-color 2½" square to a black 2½" square. Make 2.

2. Sew the two units together as shown to make the block center (Unit 1).

Unit 1

3. Sew a 2½" x 4½" black rectangle to the left and right sides of Unit 1 (Unit 2).

Unit 2

4. Sew a matching pair of 2½" x 8½" striped rectangles to the top and bottom of Unit 2 (Unit 3).

Unit 3

5. Sew a 2½" x 8½" black rectangle to the left and right sides of Unit 3 (Unit 4).

Unit 4

6. Sew a matching pair of 2½" x 12½" striped rectangles to the top and bottom of Unit 4 to complete one block.

Completed Block

7. Repeat to make a total of 30 blocks.

Quilt Layout:

Assemble the blocks into 6 rows of 5 blocks each. Sew rows together to construct the quilt body.

Border:

1. Sew together end-to-end 5 of the solid-colored 3½" x 12½" rectangles.
Make 2 Border Units using colors of your choice for the top and bottom of the quilt. Sew to the top and bottom of the quilt.

Top and Bottom

2. Sew together end-to-end 6 of the solid-colored 3½" x 12½" rectangles. Make 2 Border Units for the sides of the quilt using colors of your choice.

3. Sew a 3½" dark purple square to each end of the Side Border Units. Sew to the side of the quilt.

Both Sides

4. Layer, quilt and bind.

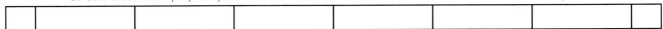

Furrows of Almolonga

Finished Quilt: 63" x 60"   Quilted By: Laura Lee Fritz

Almolonga is the largest agricultural town in the highlands. Corn of many colors and an infinite array of vegetables are grown there. It is only fitting that corn has many "earthy" tones, because it is symbolic of Mother Earth's gifts and fundamental for the Guatemalan diet. Dried corn kernels are boiled and ground to make "masa" (dough) for tortillas. It is easy for quilts to be born in this land; once you see a natural, feel-good color scheme like this, you just have to incorporate it into a quilt!

Fabric and Cutting Directions:

⅜ YD. EACH OF 22 WARM AND NEUTRAL STRIPES, PLAIDS AND ETHNIC PRINTS

- From each fabric, cut 1 strip 7¼" wide.

- Cut each strip into 4 squares 7¼" x 7¼", and cut on both diagonals.

- Cut 1 strip 3⅞" wide. Cut into 4 squares 3⅞" x 3⅞", and cut each square once across the diagonal.

3¾ YD. FABRIC FOR BACKING

½ YD. RED FABRIC FOR BINDING

- From the binding fabric, cut 6 strips 2¼" wide.

Constructing a Vertical Row:

Before piecing the rows, pre-plan the color layout (refer to the photo for inspiration). 1 row consists of 8 large triangle pairs of the 2 selected for that row, with a small triangle on each end.

1. Sew a 5⅛" triangle of one of the selected colors for a row together with a 5⅛" triangle of the other selected color as illustrated. Make 8 pairs.

2. Sew triangle pairs together to make a row as illustrated.

3. Sew a 3⅛" triangle to each end of the row to complete the row.

4. Repeat the procedure to make 21 rows.

Quilt Layout:

Sew rows together, keeping the fabric placement consistent with the original pre-planned layout.

Border:

1. Lay out the 3⅞" triangles for the top and bottom borders, using the photo as a guide for fabric placement.

2. Sew triangles together to make squares as illustrated. The top border consists of 22 squares, and the bottom border consists of 21 squares and 1 triangle.

3. Sew the 22 squares together to make the top border, and sew to the top of the quilt.

4. Sew the 21 squares and 1 triangle together to make the bottom border, and sew to the bottom of the quilt.

5. Layer, quilt and bind.

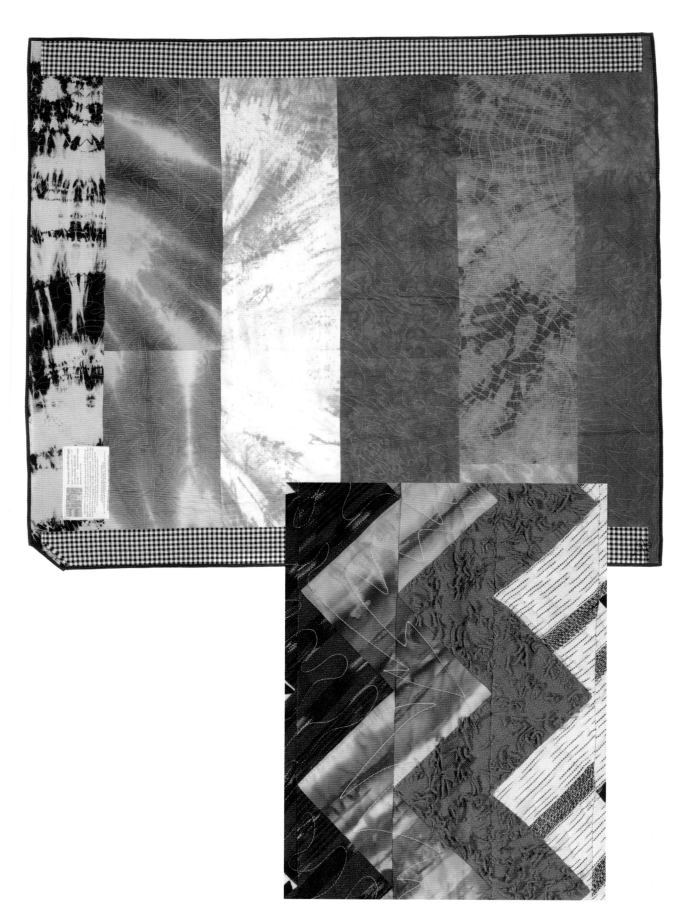

Log Cabin Sash

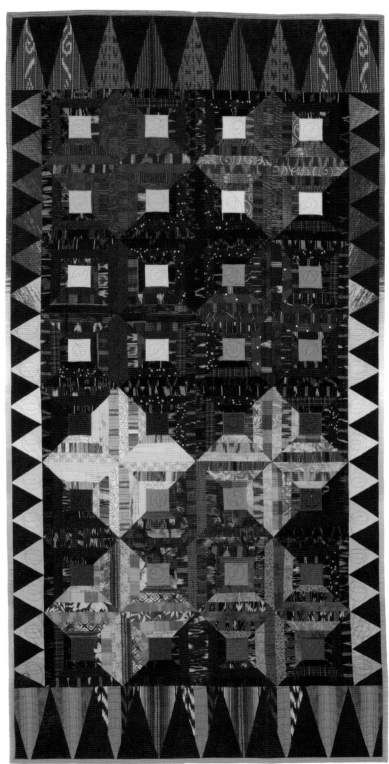

Finished Sash: 36" x 72"
Finished Block: 6¾"
Quilted By: Laura Lee Fritz

A handsome, hand-woven sash from San Pedro Sacatepéquez has been in my collection for years. It is made with heavy yarn and I just love its big, bold chunks of color. It hangs on the door of my Guatemalan fabric stash so I see it all the time. I kept wondering how I could replicate this type of pattern in a quilt, until it dawned on me: What if I made log cabin blocks, half-yellow, half-fuchsia, instead of the usual light-dark? Needless to say, a quilt was born! Many people who are intrigued by this quilt ask me how I made it, without realizing these are simple log cabin blocks with a twist!

I don't usually have the patience to make log cabin blocks in the usual manner (going round and round), so I devised a quicker method that yields perfect blocks! I call it "Perfect" Log Cabins, of course! When choosing colors for this quilt don't think about it, and don't rationalize — just go to your stash and start pulling out colors that you like. You can also use colored pencils to practice different combinations on blank diagram and see what you like best.

Fabric and Cutting Directions:

⅛ YD. EACH OF 6 DARK BLUE/NAVY FABRICS (use small prints or stripes)

⅛ YD. EACH OF 6 DARK PURPLE FABRICS (use small prints or stripes)

- From each dark blue/navy and dark purple fabric, cut 2 strips 1⅜" wide.

⅛ YD. OF 6 FABRICS OF EACH OF THE FOLLOWING COLOR GROUPS (use small prints or stripes)**: TURQUOISE, LIME, BROWN, ORANGE, YELLOW, RED, RED ORANGE, HOT PINK AND MAGENTA, FOR A TOTAL OF 54 FABRICS**

- Cut 1 strip 1⅜" wide from each of the 54 fabrics.

¼ YD. EACH OF 9 SOLIDS

- Cut 1 strip 2⅛" wide from each of the 9 solid fabrics. From each strip, cut 4 squares 2⅛" x 2⅛".
- Cut 1 strip 3½" wide from each of the 9 solid fabrics. From each strip, cut 4 Template A Triangles (for template, see pg. 81)
- Cut 1 strip 2¼" wide from each of 6 (your choice) solid fabrics for the binding.

¼ YD. OF 2 STRIPED FABRICS EACH OF GREEN, TURQUOISE AND HOT PINK AND 1 RED ORANGE (should be different fabrics than the color groups above)**, FOR A TOTAL OF 7 FABRICS.**

- Cut 1 strip 7½"-wide from each of the 7 striped fabrics, and cut 4 of Template B from each of the 7 fabrics (for template, see pg. 81)

1 YD. SOLID NAVY FABRIC

- Cut 3 strips 7½" wide, and cut into 20 of Template B.
- Cut 2 strips 3½" wide, and cut into 34 of Template A.

2 YD. FABRIC FOR BACKING

½ YD. RED FABRIC FOR BINDING

- From the binding fabric, cut 6 strips 2¼" wide.

Constructing the Log Cabin Block:

To make the log cabin blocks, divide each of the color fabric groups into Set A and Set B with three fabrics in each set. For the dark blue and purple groups only, make 2 of Set A and 2 of Set B. Division of the 6 fabrics into sets is based on personal preference.

1. Sew the 3 fabric strips of each set together to make 1 of Strip Set A and 1 of Strip Set B as illustrated.

Set A Red

Set B Red

2. Make 2 of Strip Set A and 2 of Strip Set B for the Dark Blue and Purple color groups. There will be a total of 13 of Set A and 13 of Set B.

3. Using Template C, cut each Strip Set into 8 Units.

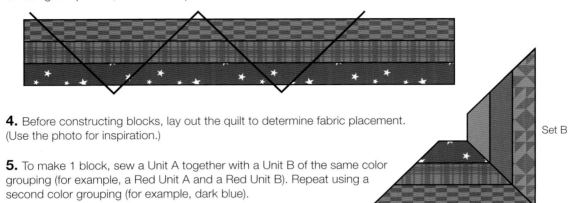

4. Before constructing blocks, lay out the quilt to determine fabric placement. (Use the photo for inspiration.)

5. To make 1 block, sew a Unit A together with a Unit B of the same color grouping (for example, a Red Unit A and a Red Unit B). Repeat using a second color grouping (for example, dark blue).

Set B

Set A

6. Sew the 2 color groupings together to form the log cabin block.

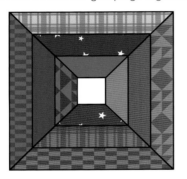

7. Assemble the Set A and Set B Units into a total of 32 blocks.

8. Pin a 2⅛" solid fabric square over the center opening of each block, making sure that all 4 of the inner edges are covered. Satin stitch the square in place using matching thread.

Quilt Layout:

1. Sew blocks into 8 rows of 4 blocks each.
2. Sew the rows together to complete the body of the quilt.

Borders:

Pre-plan color placement before sewing triangles together.

Side Borders

1. Sew 17 of Navy Templates A to 16 of Solid Template A as illustrated.

Make 2

2. Mark the center of the border unit and the center of the quilt sides.

3. Matching the center points, pin borders to the sides of the quilt, making sure that the solid colored triangle bases are against the side of the quilt. Sew and trim each border unit even with the top and bottom of the quilt.

Top and Bottom Borders

1. Sew 10 of Navy Template B to 9 of striped Template B.

2. Repeat directions for sewing on the side border. Match centers and trim border ends with the side of the quilt.

3. Layer, quilt and bind.

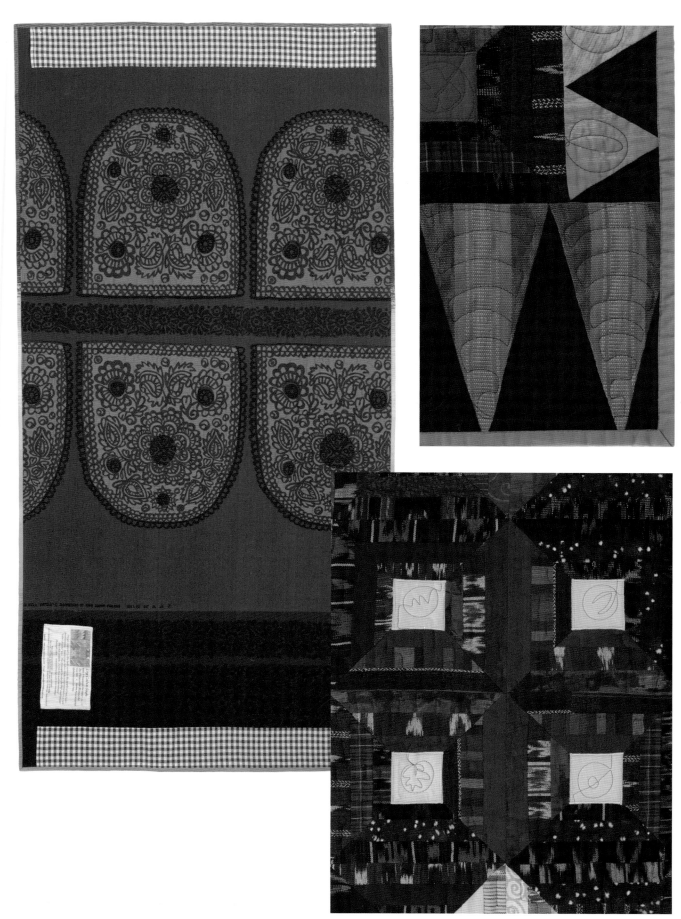

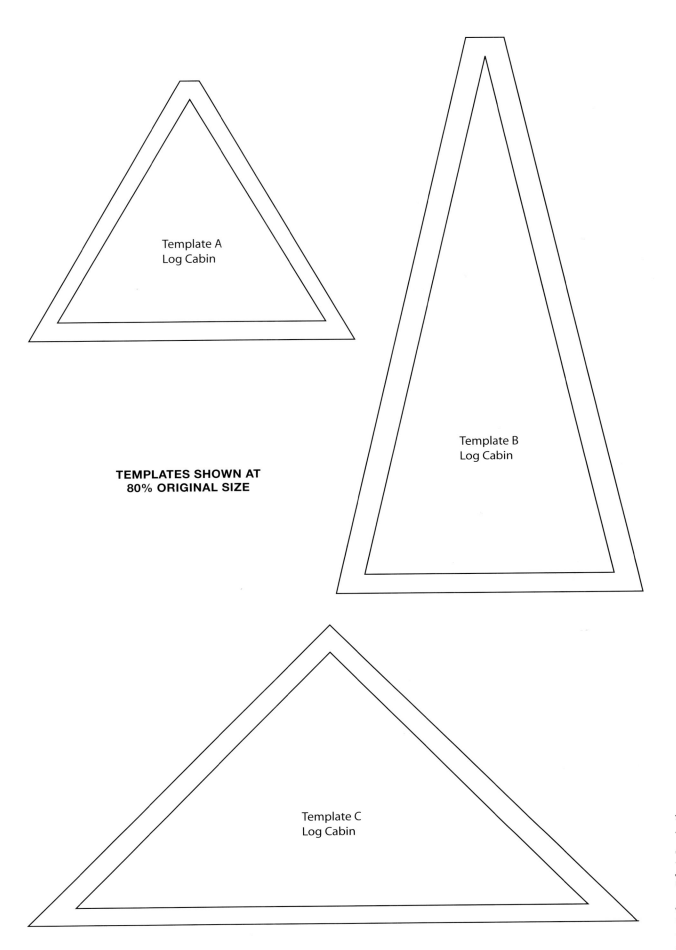

Template A
Log Cabin

Template B
Log Cabin

**TEMPLATES SHOWN AT
80% ORIGINAL SIZE**

Template C
Log Cabin

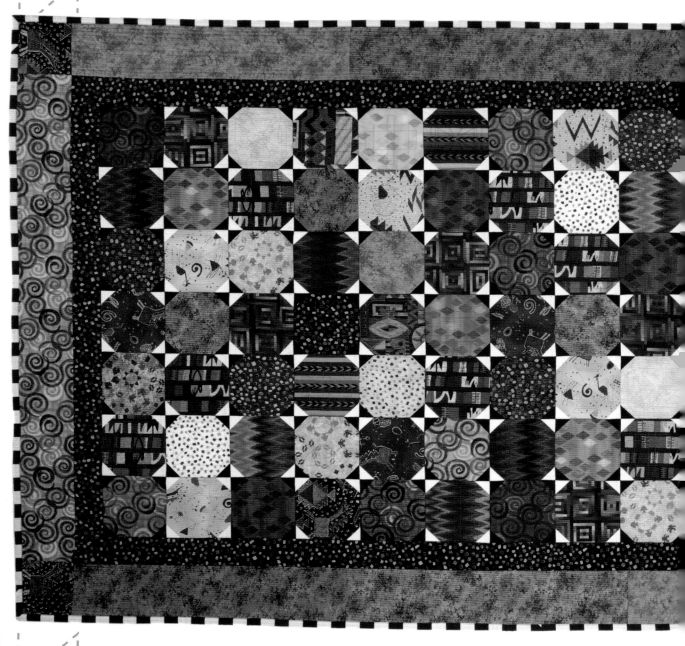

Colors of San Antonio

Finished Quilt: 43½" x 66"   Finished Block: 4½"   Quilted By: Peg Spradlin

The women from San Antonio Aguas Calientes are known for weaving one of the finest brocades in the country. I was inspired by a huipil's detailed pattern to make a quilt that would showcase my first fabric collection for Robert Kaufman. The collection, which premiered in the fall of 2004, was based on Guatemalan textiles, and I wanted a simple design that would let the fabric be the main attraction. The large area in the center of each Snowball block is perfect to display any collection of gorgeous 4" or 5" fabric squares. The black-and-white corners of the blocks, which form hourglass shapes, will give any fabrics you use enough "breathing" space for an effective visual balance.

Fabric and Cutting Directions:

⅜ YD. EACH OF 12 COLORFUL FABRICS OF YOUR CHOICE

- Cut 1 strip 5" wide from each of the fabrics. Cut each strip into 8 squares 5" x 5". (The quilt uses 84 squares. There are more squares than needed to allow for different layout choices.)
- Choose 9 of the fabrics and cut 1 strip 4½" wide from each for the second border.

⅜ YD. WHITE FABRIC

- Cut 7 strips 1½" wide. Cut into 168 squares 1½" x 1½".

⅞ YD. BLACK FABRIC

- Cut 7 strips 1½" wide. Cut into 168 squares 1½" x 1½".

⅝ YD. DARK PRINT FABRIC

- Cut 6 strips 2½" wide for the first border.

½ YD. FABRIC FOR BINDING

- Cut 6 strips 2¼" wide.

2¾ YD. FABRIC FOR BACKING

Do Not Cut

Tip

After cutting 5" squares, separate them into two groups. Make Group 1 (calm) small to medium prints, tone on tone, geometric, etc. These squares will have white corners. Make Group 2 (busy) medium to large patterns, theme prints, wide stripes, etc. These squares will have black corners. Separating fabric squares allows for a balanced arrangement.

Constructing Blocks:

1. Draw a diagonal line on the reverse side of the 1½" black and white squares.

2. Place 4 squares (same color) on the four corners of one of the 5" squares. Sew on the drawn line. Cut ¼" away from the sewing line, and press as illustrated.

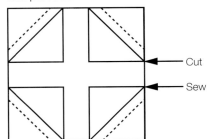

Cut

Sew

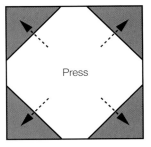

Press

3. Make 42 blocks with black corner squares and 42 with white corner squares.

Quilt Layout:

Using the photo, lay out blocks to construct the quilt top. There will be 12 rows of 7 blocks each.

Border:

Measure the quilt body — if your measurements are different, cut to your measurements.

1st Border

1. Cut 2 of the 2½" wide strips down to measure 2½" x 32", and sew to the top and bottom of the quilt.

2. Sew 2 of the 2½" wide strips together end-to-end. Repeat to make two sets.

3. Cut the strips down to measure 58½" long, and sew to the sides of the quilt.

2nd Border

1. Cut 2 of the 4½" wide strips down to measure 4½" x 36", and sew to the top and bottom of the quilt.

2. Cut 6 of the 4½" strips to measure 4½" x 20".

3. Sew 3 of the 4½" x 20" strips together end to end. Repeat to make two sets.

4. Trim each set down to measure 4½" x 58½".

5. From the last 4½" strip, cut 4 squares 4½" x 4½".

6. Sew the 4½" squares to each end of the 58½"-long side border strips.

7. Sew to the sides of the quilt.

8. Layer, quilt and bind.

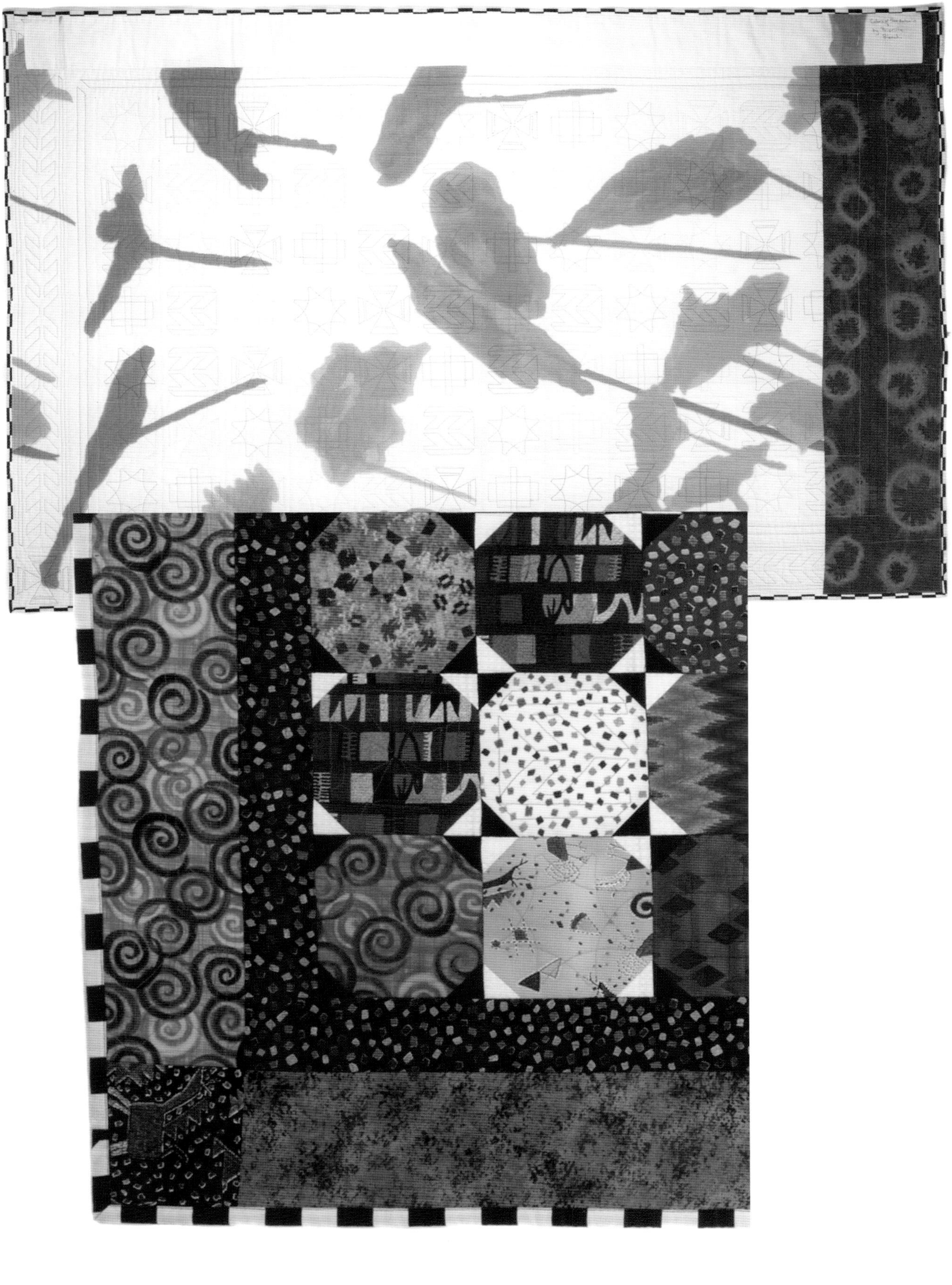

Eye Candy

Finished Quilt: 40" x 60"   Finished Block: 7"   Quilted By: Laura Lee Fritz

Rosary candies, for sale at the market by Amatitlan Lake, were one of our favorite treats when we were kids! The whole time I was making this quilt, I kept thinking about them, and I began to wonder why. Maybe the brightly colored corn husk wrappers, mostly in shades of hot pink and turquoise, are behind the inspiration for this quilt. Or maybe seeing the design's rounded shapes with a yummy center had something to do with it. In any case, I made the quilt with a happy heart and a smile on my face, and I am sure you will do the same!

Fabric and Cutting Directions:

¼ YD. EACH 13 STRIPED FABRICS FOR BLOCK TRIANGLES

- Cut 1 strip 5¾" wide of each fabric. Cut into 7 squares 5¾" x 5¾". Cut across both diagonals. Use only the triangles in which the stripe is horizontal to the base of the triangle. The remaining triangles are not used in this project. Save them for another quilt.

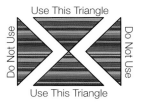

¼ YD. EACH 13 STRIPED AND PLAID FABRICS FOR BLOCK CENTERS

- Cut 1 strip 4" wide from each of the block center fabrics. Cut 7 of Template A from each strip (for template, see pg. 88).

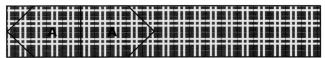

½ YD. VARIEGATED FABRIC FOR BINDING

- Cut 6 strips 2¼" wide.

1⅞ YD. FABRIC FOR BACKING

Constructing Blocks:

Before constructing the blocks, lay out the quilt to determine fabric color placement.

1. Sew 2 Template A pieces together as illustrated to make a Block Center Unit.

Block Center Unit

2. Fold 2 corner triangles in half and finger press. Mark the center of the base.

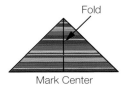

Fold

Mark Center

3. Align the center of the triangle base with the seam joining the 2 fabrics of the Block Center Unit. Sew 1 triangle to each side of the Block Center Unit as illustrated.

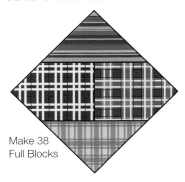

Make 38
Full Blocks

Constructing Setting Triangles:

1. Sew a triangle to both sides of a Template A piece as illustrated.

2. Trim the triangles even with the base of the Template A.

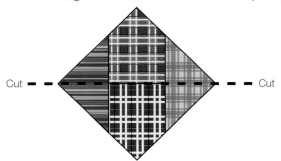

Cut — — — — — — Cut

Constructing Quilt:

1. Sew blocks together in 10 diagonal rows as illustrated.

2. Sew rows together to complete quilt top.

3. Layer, quilt and bind.

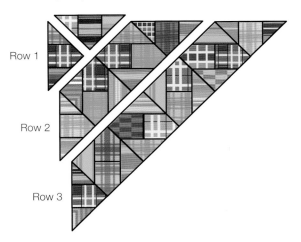

Row 1

Row 2

Row 3

Eye Candy
Template A

Holiday in Nebaj IV

Finished Quilt: 39" x 39"   Finished Block: 6" x 6"   Quilted By: Priscilla Bianchi

Three spectacular hand-woven belts from the town of Nebaj inspired this design. I enjoy creating as many diamond variations in my quilts as I possibly can imagine. This project is an incredibly simple-to-make quilt that looks complex, intriguing and stunning! It is a perfect example of how stripes do not have to match to look good in a quilt. I especially love the optical illusions created by the stripes coming together into squares, and the now-you-see-it-now-you-don't effect that it generates.

Fabric and Cutting Directions:

⅜ YD. EACH 12 DIFFERENT STRIPED FABRICS (make sure to use different values of light, medium and dark to add interest)

- Cut 1 strip 9¾" wide. Cut each strip into 4 squares 9¾" x 9¾". Cut each square across both diagonals. Use only the triangles in which the stripe is horizontal to the base of the triangle. The remaining triangles are not used in this project. Save them for another quilt.

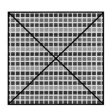 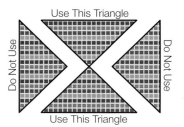

⅜ YD. BLUE SOLID FABRIC FOR FIRST BORDER

- Cut 4 strips 2½" wide.

½ YD. FABRIC FOR BINDING

- Cut 5 strips 2¼" wide.

1¼ YD. FABRIC FOR BACKING

Constructing Blocks and Body of Quilt:

Pre-plan color layout before constructing blocks.

1. Sew 2 triangles of different fabrics together to make a square as illustrated.

2. Repeat to make 36 blocks.

3. Sew 4 blocks together to form an X design, as illustrated. Make 9 X Units.

4. Sew the X Units together into 3 rows of 3 units each.

5. Sew rows together.

Border:

1. Cut, measure and sew 2 of the 2¼" strips to the top and bottom of the quilt.

2. Cut, measure and sew the 2 remaining 2¼" strips to the sides of the quilt.

3. Layer, quilt and bind.

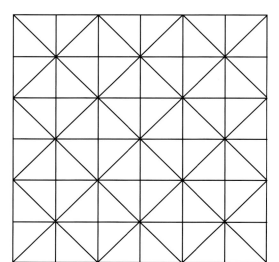

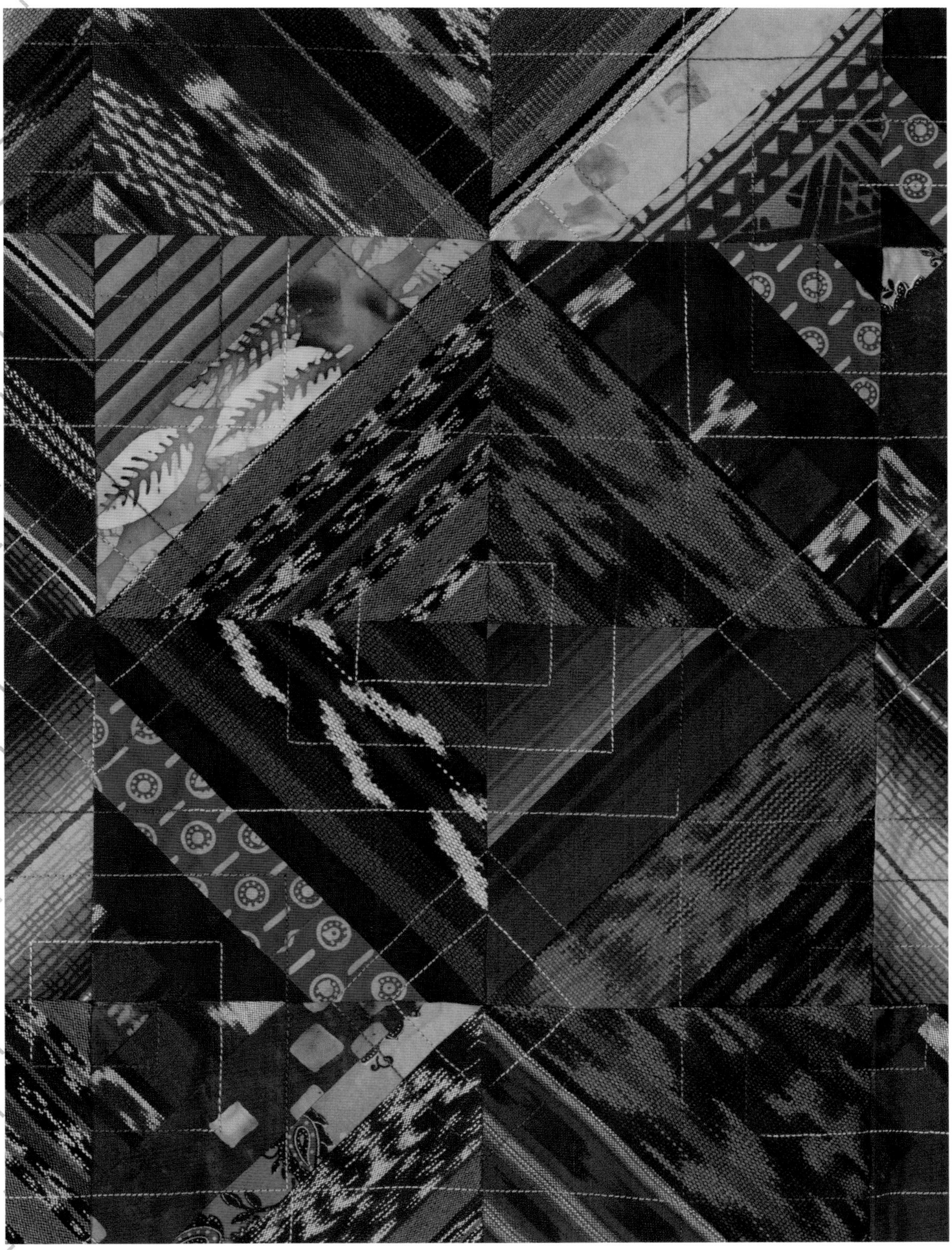

Glowing Stars

Finished Quilt: 52½" x 57"   Quilted By: Christine's Custom Quilts

The large, stunning stars in a huipil from Almolonga attracted my creative spirit like a magnet. I just had to make a quilt with stars to the max! After sketching and trying out different styles of stars — 8-pointed (too chubby), Lemoyne (too hard to make), paper pieced (too boring) — I settled for this vibrant, hexagonal 6-sided pieced star, which I love! I used 50% Guatemalan hand-wovens and 50% commercial fabrics for a lively, overall balanced look.

Fabric and Cutting Directions:

⅜ YD. EACH 17 TONE-ON-TONE PRINTS

⅜ YD. EACH 17 STRIPED OR PLAID FABRICS

- Cut 2 strips 3" wide of each tone-on-tone and striped/plaid fabric.

¾ YD. DARK BLUE FABRIC

- Cut 2 strips 4" wide, and cut into 28 of Template B triangles.
- Cut 6 strips 2" wide for the first border.

½ YD. FABRIC FOR BINDING

3¾ YD. FABRIC FOR BACKING

Construction:

1. Pair up one tone-on-tone strip with a striped fabric strip. With strips right sides together, sew together lengthwise. Make a second strip set with the same tone-on-tone and stripe fabric. Repeat with the 16 remaining tone-on-tone and striped fabrics. There will be a total of 32 strip sets, 2 of each fabric combination.

Make 2 of Each Color Grouping

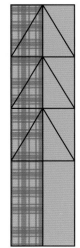

2. With the striped fabric on the left and the tone-on-tone on the right, place the center line of Template A on the strip set seam. Cut 9 of Template A from each strip set (for template, see pg. 96).

3. Cut 1 strip 2¾" wide of each tone-on-tone and striped/plaid fabric. Cut each strip into 13 squares 2¾" x 2¾" (more than needed).

Constructing Stars:

1. Sew Template A Star Points together as illustrated.

2. Make 6 Half Star Units of each color grouping. Do not sew Half Star Units together.

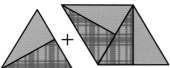

Constructing Quilt:

1. Assemble the body of the quilt using the 98 Half Star Units for a total of 46 complete stars and 6 half stars. Lay out all of the Half Star Units and the Template B background triangles in horizontal rows.

2. Ensure that the 2 Half Star Units of the same color will form a complete star when rows are sewn together. Arrange the different colored stars until you are pleased with the arrangement.

3. Sew together in horizontal rows. There will be a total of 14 rows.

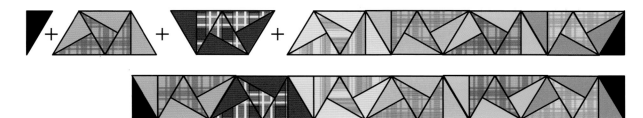

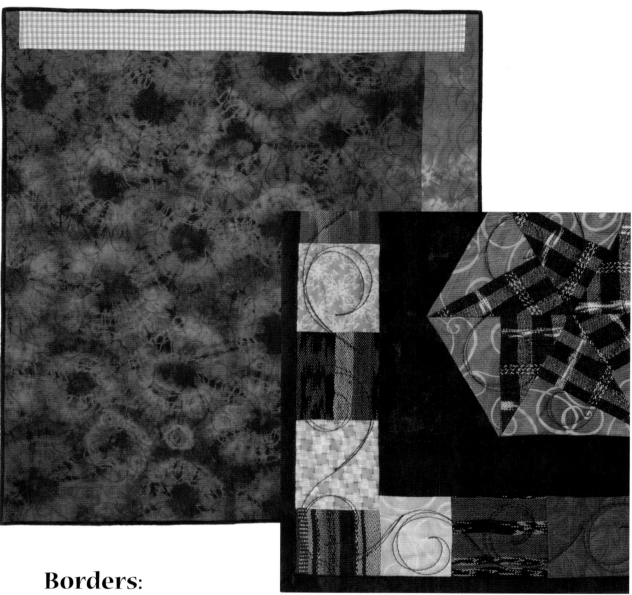

Borders:
1st Border

1. Cut 1 of the 2" wide dark blue border strips in half width wise to make 2 strips 2" x 21".

2. Sew a 2" x 21" strip end-to-end to a 2" x 42" strip. Repeat to make 2 long strips. Cut each to fit the width of the quilt, and sew to the top and bottom of the quilt.

3. Repeat steps 1 and 2 for the sides of the quilt. Cut to the length of the quilt and sew to the sides.

2nd Border

1. Using your choice of colors, sew enough 2¾" squares together to measure the width of the quilt. Make 2. If the strips are too long, trim to fit and sew to the top and bottom of the quilt.

2. Repeat step 1 for the sides of the quilt. Cut to fit the length of the quilt and sew to the sides.

3. Layer, quilt and bind.

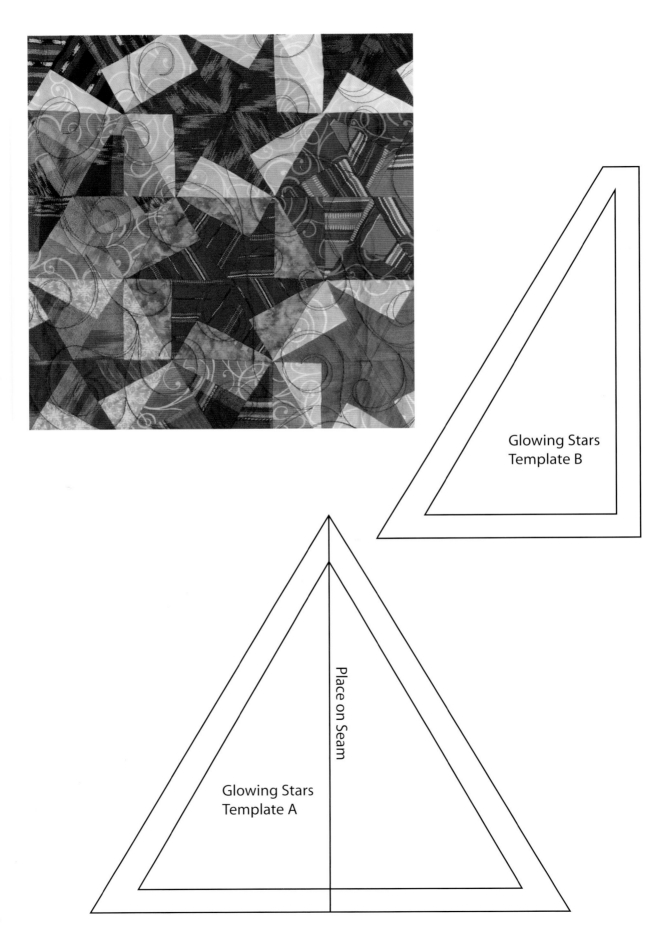

Glowing Stars
Template B

Place on Seam

Glowing Stars
Template A

Flora

Finished Quilt: 68" x 59"   Finished Patch: 3" x 3"   Quilted By: Priscilla Bianchi

A collar from the huipil of San Cristóbal Totonicapán displays an abundance of multi-colored flowers that mirrors the area's natural exuberance. This hand-embroidered masterpiece inspired me to create a charm quilt which resembles the same type of repetitive pattern. One shape — the tumbler — is used throughout, repeated over and over in a zillion colors and textures!

The Flora Quilt uses all 12 colors on the color wheel. More than eight fabrics per color can be used. Four-inch to six-inch squares, Charm Squares or scraps will also work for this quilt.

Fabric and Cutting Directions:

⅛ YD. EACH OF 8 DIFFERENT FABRICS FOR EACH OF THE FOLLOWING COLORS:
red, red-violet, violet, blue-violet, blue, blue-green, green, yellow-green, yellow, yellow-orange, orange and red-orange, for a total of 96 fabrics. Use a variety of stripes, prints and solids with light, medium and dark values.

- Cut 1 strip 3½" wide from each of the 96 fabrics.

- Cut 4 Template A, 1 Template B and 1 Template B reverse from each strip (see template pattern on pg. 100). To cut the Template B reverse, flip the template and place it right-side down on the fabric, or fold the fabric wrong sides together and cut 1 Template B. Each cut will yield 1 B and 1 B reverse.

¼ YD. OF 13 FABRICS FOR THE BORDER (see quilt photo)

- Cut 1 strip 6" wide of each fabric.

⅝ YD. FABRIC FOR BINDING (or use scraps of different leftover fabrics and piece together enough scraps to bind the quilt)

- Cut 7 strips 2¼" wide.

3¾ YD. FABRIC FOR BACKING

> **Tip**
> Try placing all of the lights of all colors in the upper third of the quilt, and then position medium values in the middle third and dark values on the bottom third.

Construction:

1. Arrange the fabrics by color into 12 piles. Using the color photo as a guide, lay out the pieces in rows. Each row will contain 24 of Template A, 1 Template B, and 1 Template B reverse. Continue laying out the quilt until there are 16 rows.

2. Sew the rows together to make the body of the quilt.

Borders:
Top Border

1. Cut 4 of the 6" wide border strips into 4 different lengths, making sure that when they are sewn together end-to-end they are at least 72" long.

Bottom Border

1. Repeat directions for the top border using 3 fabrics.

Side Borders

1. For each of the side borders, cut 3 of the remaining 6" border strips into 3 different lengths, making sure that when they are sewn together end-to-end they are at least 62" long.

Sewing Border to Quilt

1. Fold each border strip in half to find the center, and finger press.

2. Match the center point on the border strip to the center of the quilt, and pin.

3. Sew each border strip to the quilt, starting and stopping ¼" in from the edge of the quilt.

4. Miter corners.

5. Layer, quilt and bind.

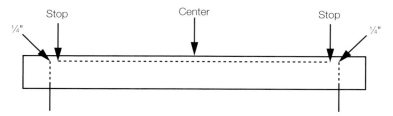

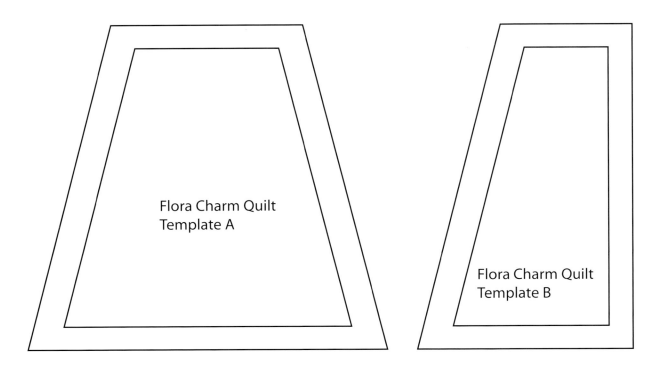

Flora Charm Quilt
Template A

Flora Charm Quilt
Template B

Starbursts Go Red Hot

Finished Quilt: 39" x 49" Finished Block: 8" x 9" Quilted By: Priscilla Bianchi

Even though we do not have a quilting tradition in Guatemala, quilting imagery, motifs and patterns are everywhere. Take for instance a flower rug, freshly made in the wee hours of the morning along the religious procession's path as a reverence to the Virgin Mary. It looks just like eight-pointed stars, hexagon flowers or Grandma's Garden blocks! The "starbursts" in this quilt are made by piecing together six kite-shaped patches into a hexagon. The color scheme takes your breath away!

Fabric and Cutting Directions:

⅜ YD. EACH OF LIGHT YELLOW AND DARK BLUE FABRIC

- Cut 2 strips 5¼" wide of the light yellow and dark blue fabrics (for the first and last row).

- Cut each strip into 11 of Template A, 1 of Template B, and 1 of Template B reverse (for templates, see pg. 105)

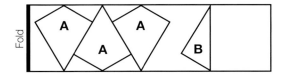

¼ YD. EACH OF 20 STRIPED AND PRINTED FABRICS IN A VARIETY OF YELLOW, ORANGE, RED AND PURPLE. (The amount of fabric needed is based on achieving a similar look to the actual quilt. Depending on the repeats of the stripes or pattern in the fabric, the amount of fabric may need to be doubled to achieve the needed placement of templates.)

- Cut 1 strip 5¼" wide of each of the 20 fabrics.

- From 18 of the strips (complete starburst units), cut 6 of Template A.

- From the 2 remaining strips (half starburst units), cut 4 of Template A, 2 of Template B and 2 of Template B reverse. To cut reverse templates, flip the template right-side down and cut, or fold fabric wrong sides together and cut one Template B. Each cut will yield 1 B and 1 B reverse.

1½ YD. VARIEGATED FABRIC FOR BINDING AND BORDER

- Cut 4 strips 5" wide for border (extra yardage allowed for color placement).

- Cut 7 strips 2¼" wide for binding.

1⅝ YD. FABRIC FOR BACKING

Constructing the Quilt:

Place all of the pieces on the design wall. Adjust arrangement unit until the design is pleasing.

1. From the light yellow and dark blue fabrics, make 1 Corner Unit, 1 Corner Reverse and 3 Half Starburst Units of each color as illustrated.

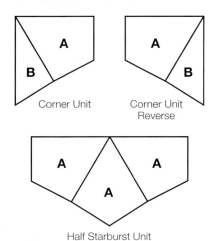

2. From the 18 colors chosen for the Complete Starburst Unit, make 18 Starburst as illustrated.

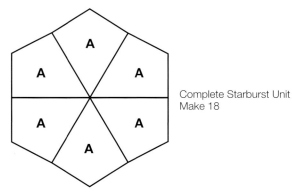

Complete Starburst Unit
Make 18

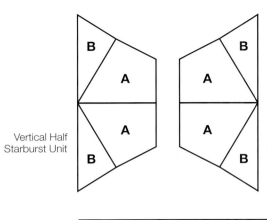

Vertical Half
Starburst Unit

A **A** **B** **B** **A** **A** **B** **B**

Vertical Half
Starburst Unit Reverse

3. From the 2 colors chosen for
the Vertical Half Starburst Units,
make 1 Unit and 1 Unit Reverse
from each color.

4. Sew blocks into rows. Sew to dot
(DO NOT sew through seam allowance).

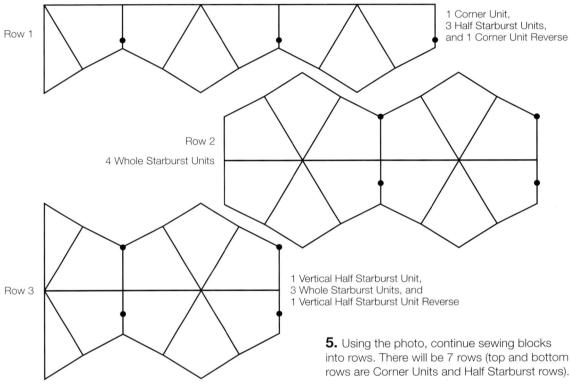

Row 1

1 Corner Unit,
3 Half Starburst Units,
and 1 Corner Unit Reverse

Row 2
4 Whole Starburst Units

Row 3

1 Vertical Half Starburst Unit,
3 Whole Starburst Units, and
1 Vertical Half Starburst Unit Reverse

5. Using the photo, continue sewing blocks
into rows. There will be 7 rows (top and bottom
rows are Corner Units and Half Starburst rows).

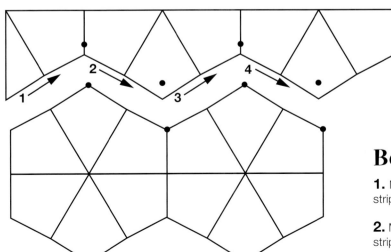

6. Sew rows into quilt body,
setting in hexagons as illustrated.
Sew to dot, stop, and backstitch.
Start at dot, and sew to next dot;
backstitch. Continue to the end
of the row. DO NOT sew through
the seam allowance to the dots.

Border

1. Measure, cut and sew 2 of the 5"-wide
strips to the sides of the quilt.

2. Measure, cut and sew 2 of the 5"-wide
strips to the top and bottom of the quilt.

3. Layer, quilt and bind.

Starbursts Go Red Hot
Template B

Starbursts Go Red Hot
Template A

Chapter 6 **La Galería**

From 1998 (Series I):

"Forms & Colors Dancing on Fabric"

My first series of art quilts consists of 17 pieces created between October 1997 and February 1999. During this time, I focused on learning an array of different techniques. Even at this early stage in my career, and although I found it necessary to stay close to tradition in order to learn, my free spirit and distinctive style was beginning to emerge.

1. "Earth Tones"
(Tonos Tierra) 46" x 46"

MATERIALS: U.S. commercial cottons and Indonesian batiks
TECHNIQUE: Machine pieced and free-motion quilted

This is one of the first pieces I made as I was learning to quilt, following instructions from "Scrap Quilts Fast and Fun" (Oxmoor House). The simple yet effective geometric design is a contemporary showcase of all the many hues that make up the "earth" tones. I spiced it up by adding Indonesian batiks and sparks of bright Chinese red! I also deepened some of the values in the background triangles to obtain a higher contrast. It's a favorite! *Photo, Rolando Bianchi.*

2. "Venetian Marble"
(Mármol de Venecia) 30" x 30"

MATERIALS: U.S. commercial cottons and marbled fabrics
TECHNIQUE: Machine pieced and free-motion quilted

Although I wasn't aware of this before I started quilting, I find geometric designs irresistible. I love the order and neatness of repetitive patterns, and I have always been attracted by mosaics and floor tile designs. This quilt came from Kaffe Fassett's "Glorious Patchwork" book, which was inspired by antique mosaic tiles on the floor of St. Mark's Cathedral in Venice, Italy. *Photo, Rolando Bianchi.*

3. "Warm Hearted"
(De Corazón Cálido) 33" x 49"

MATERIALS: U.S. commercial cottons and Indonesian batiks
TECHNIQUE: Machine pieced and quilted

This is a "charm quilt" made of 250 half-hexagons cut from 250 different fabrics in warm hues. This traditional (and at the same time, very contemporary) design assumes that there is a source of light at the top of the quilt, thus creating the optical illusion of volume, depth and perspective. It's amazing to see how fabric can give so much light, and how a flat surface can look so three-dimensional! *Photo, Rolando Bianchi.*

4. "Cool Attitude"
(De Actitud Fresca) 33" x 49"

MATERIALS: U.S. commercial cottons and Indonesian batiks
TECHNIQUE: Machine pieced and quilted

This charm quilt, made of 250 half-hexagons, was cut from 250 different fabrics in cool hues. This design assumes that there is a source of light at the top of the quilt, thus creating the optical illusion of volume, depth and perspective. Two quilts cut from the same design can look so different! *Photo, Rolando Bianchi.*

5. "1,000 Rainbow Pyramids"
(1,000 Pirámides Arcoiris) 42" x 71"

MATERIALS: U.S. commercial cottons and Indonesian batiks
TECHNIQUE: Machine pieced and quilted

To make this charm quilt, I cut one pyramid (60° triangle) shape from every single fabric in my stash at the time. There are 480 different triangles, and not one fabric repeats itself. This piece is not only a visual delight, but it is also a wonderful journey into color. Your eyes glide over the surface as one color transitions into the next, and the next, and the next, until you've traveled the entire color spectrum. *Photo, Rolando Bianchi.*

6. "Four Color Pinwheel"

(Rehilete de Cuatro Colores) 32" x 32"

MATERIALS: U.S. commercial cottons and Indonesian batiks
TECHNIQUE: Machine pieced and quilted

I love the order of this design with its neat lines and angles. Being a fabric lover it's wonderful to have such a valid excuse to include hundreds of different fabrics in just one quilt. There are 200 different 45° triangle-shaped pieces; no two patches are alike! *Photo, Rolando Bianchi.*

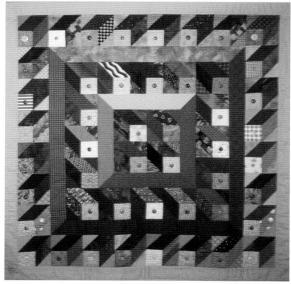

7. "Roman Quartz"

(Cuarzo Romano) 51" x 51"

MATERIALS: U.S. commercial cottons and Indonesian batiks
TECHNIQUE: Machine pieced, fusible appliquéd and free-motion quilted

This is an exciting quilt that sizzles! The bold, vibrant colors have been combined in a way that creates harmony and balance. The inner turquoise and violet borders were necessary to "cool down" the strong, warm blocks. The outer gold border ties everything together, creating a fitting frame. The pattern reminds me of building blocks, and it is derived from a design by Kaffe Fassett. *Photo, Rolando Bianchi.*

8. "Lone Star"

(Estrella Solitaria) 52" x 52"

MATERIALS: U.S. commercial cottons
TECHNIQUE: Machine pieced and quilted

This traditional American pattern also known as the "Star of Bethlehem," is the most traditional quilt I made as I was learning an array of quilting techniques. Sewing and keeping all those bias edges straight was difficult, and it taught me to appreciate the hand work and skill evident in historic quilts.

Since mixing blue and yellow results in green, deep green was the logical choice for the four corner blocks. I couldn't resist using an unusual floral background to give it a twist! *Photo, Rolando Bianchi.*

9. "Undulating Rainbow I"
(Arcoiris Ondulante I) 55" x 55"

10. "Undulating Rainbow II"
Arcoiris Ondulante II) 55" x 55"

MATERIALS: U.S. commercial cottons, plaids and Indonesian batiks
TECHNIQUE: Machine pieced and quilted

This art quilt began as a vision of colors and forms dancing in my mind. I've always been attracted to the wondrous range of colors in the rainbow, and I will use the whole spectrum whenever the design allows it! I also enjoy making something simple that looks complex and keeps people wondering, "How'd she do that?" My creative juices went wild as I flipped through the pages in Margaret Miller's "Blockbender Quilts" book ... to create the optical illusion of curves in a quilt by sewing only straight seams ... How neat can this be? I just had do it!

This wavy effect makes me think of soft, wavy clouds at sundown or soft wind swaying the trees in a forest, and a rapid river flowing or a waterfall cascading into waves of white foam. *Photo, Rolando Bianchi.*

11. "Blue & White Kaleidoscope"
(Caleidoscopio Azul y Blanco) 50" x 50"

MATERIALS: U.S. commercial cottons and Indonesian batiks
TECHNIQUE: Machine pieced and free-motion quilted

I made this kaleidoscope medallion quilt from eight identical, symmetrical wedges. Each wedge is made up of hundreds of pieces, some as small as ½". The traditional monochromatic blue-and-white color scheme gave me an elegant, pleasing design suggestive of lace, fine things and romance. The border fabric took my breath away; I cut a very wide border so as not to break up its fantastic pattern. *Photo, Rolando Bianchi.*

12. "Purple Dance Kaleidoscope"
(Caleidoscopio Danza Púrpura) 41" x 41"

MATERIALS: U.S. commercial cottons, Indonesian batiks and Japanese yukatas
TECHNIQUE: Machine pieced and quilted

This kaleidoscope – medallion quilt is made from eight identical, symmetrical wedges. Each wedge is made up of hundreds of pieces, some as small as ½". The fine detail and the color scheme in deep, dramatic jewel tones produced a sophisticated, elegant design. I love how the dark background makes the center stand out; it appears as if you are looking through an actual kaleidoscope. The light that appears to be coming from within gives the design a crystalline quality. *Photo, Rolando Bianchi.*

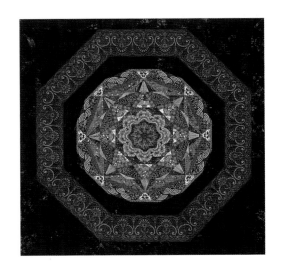

13. "Stained Glass Kaleidoscope"
(Caleidoscopio de Vitral) 46" x 46"

MATERIALS: U.S. commercial cottons and Indonesian batiks
TECHNIQUE: Machine pieced and quilted

This kaleidoscope medallion quilt was made from eight identical, symmetrical wedges. Each wedge is made up of hundreds of pieces, some as small as ½". This quilt reminds me of richly decorated stained glass windows in Gothic cathedrals. Just as in a kaleidoscope, the flower-like design opens up and gives the impression that it will be changing again any second now.

The Indian-style large print I used for the petals is so rich that it seems to have come directly from the Maharajah's palace. The scrumptious color scheme in jewel tones suggests a touch of the Orient. *Photo, Rolando Bianchi.*

From 1999 (Series II):

"Art Quilts From Guatemalan Folklore"

After having mastered technique and achieving excellence in workmanship, I channeled all my creative energy into design. This second group of art quilts reflects my experimentation with the richness of Guatemalan textiles, colors, patterns and symbolism to flavor these quilts with magic, mystical Mayan culture. *Photo, Rolando Bianchi.*

14. "My Home's Patio"
(El Patio de mi Casa) 56" x 46"

MATERIALS: Guatemalan hand-woven textiles, African, Indonesian and commercial cottons
TECHNIQUE: Machine pieced, fusible appliquéd and free-motion quilted

When working with precious ethnic textiles, use fabric in large chunks instead of cutting it up into tiny bits as you would for traditional quilt patterns. This will show off unique, hand-made qualities.

My goal here was to blend a wide variety of rustic, hand-made fabrics into an interesting background arrangement. I also wanted to depart from the accurate geometric blocks I mostly work with and experiment with improvisational piecing. I was deeply moved and inspired by Roberta Horton's "The Fabric Makes the Quilt" book. *Photo, Rolando Bianchi. Quilted by Laura Lee Fritz.*

15. "Dancing Lions and Zebras"
(Leones y Cebras Danzando) 49" x 36"

MATERIALS: Guatemalan hand-woven textiles, African, Indonesian and commercial cottons
TECHNIQUE: Machine pieced, fusible appliquéd and free-motion quilted

The fabric made me do this whimsical design! This is one of the first quilts I made using ethnic fabrics, and I absolutely loved it. The process of just cutting spontaneously without accurate measuring turned out to be relaxing and fun. The mischievous lions came from a linen blend dress that was hanging in my closet; I had to cut it — and they were the perfect finishing touch! You can almost feel the lions jumping around in their hand-woven, hand-printed fabric jungle. *Photo, Rolando Bianchi.*

16. "Lightning By Day"
(Relámpago de Día) 54" x 47"

MATERIALS: Guatemalan hand-woven textiles, Indonesian batiks and commercial cottons
TECHNIQUE: Machine pieced and free-motion quilted

Geometric zigzag patterns of Pre-Hispanic origins are widely used in Guatemalan Mayan textiles. This motif appears over and over in my work; I love its strong visual impact and the movement it conveys.

The Mayan zigzag pattern will take on different meanings, depending on the town it originates from. In this quilt, I tried to capture the meaning of lightning. In other cases, the pattern may represent a sacred snake, the footpaths left behind when climbing up steep mountains, or the highs and lows in a woman's life. The warm colors evoke a hot, sunny day. *Photo, Rolando Bianchi.*

17. "Lightning By Night"
(Relámpago de Noche) 54" x 47"

MATERIALS: Guatemalan hand-woven textiles, Indonesian batiks and commercial cottons
TECHNIQUE: Machine pieced and free-motion quilted

The Mayan zigzag pattern in this quilt represents lightning as well, and the cool palette evokes a cool breezy night up in the highlands. *Photo, Rolando Bianchi.*

18. "Flora"
68" x 59"

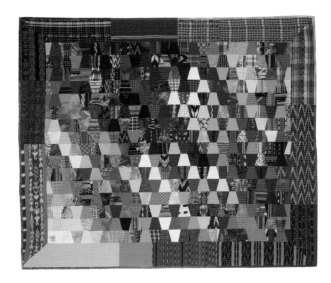

MATERIALS: Guatemalan hand-woven textiles, Indonesian batiks and commercial cottons

TECHNIQUE: Machine pieced and free-motion quilted

A charm quilt is traditionally made by cutting all your pieces into one single shape. In this case, I used a flat-tipped triangular shape known as "tumbler." The kicker is to cut each piece from a different fabric, so no two patches are alike! There are more than 400 different fabrics in this quilt, about half of which are ethnic, hand-woven Mayan textiles. For added variety and visual interest, I mixed-and-matched them with other commercial fabrics and Indonesian batiks. Many times, the work will suggest its own name. Putting together all these bright patches reminded me of the richness and profusion of multicolor flowers in Guatemala. *Photo, Rolando Bianchi.*

19. "Fauna"
59" x 59"

MATERIALS: Guatemalan hand-woven textiles, African, Indonesian and commercial cottons

TECHNIQUE: Machine pieced and free-motion quilted

Guatemala's northern territory extends from the Yucatan Peninsula. This is where all our ancient Maya cities (like Tikal) are located. These flatlands have a hot, humid climate and are covered by thick jungle.

This quilt is appropriately named for the many animals that inhabit this tropical rainforest. If you listen closely, you can almost hear them! I used all the animal skin fabrics I could find to give it more realism. This fabric mix resulted in wonderful "earthy" tones, with rich golds and splashes of black and white in just the right places.

I learned the cutting/block technique from "Easy Pieces," by Margaret Miller. *Photo, Rolando Bianchi.*

20. "Black Coffee"
(Café Negro) 52" x 67"

MATERIALS: Guatemalan hand-woven textiles, Indonesian batik panel, "Op-Art" black & white and other U.S. commercial cottons

TECHNIQUE: Machine pieced and quilted

The central batik panel started it all. I had it for years, and every now and then I'd pull it out, unfold it, drape it and caress it ... but I would carefully put it away again, not knowing what to do with it. Then suddenly one day I realized it could be used whole! My heart beat faster as I started to sketch different ideas. Soon thereafter, I was pulling out more fabrics and cutting away!

This exotic-looking quilt combines a wonderful variety of textures in rich colors of gold, brown and red. The unexpected combination with black & white op-art details balances the design, and the triangular shapes tie it together in a harmonious way. There's a mysterious feel to it.

One of the qualities of Guatemalan textiles I like the most is their versatility. They take on new personalities; in this piece they evoke a feeling of Africa ... or perhaps an Oriental rug! *Photo, Rolando Bianchi.*

21. "Chajul"
26" x 58"

MATERIALS: Guatemalan hand-woven textiles and commercial cottons
TECHNIQUE: Machine pieced and quilted

With this design, I began a series of quilts inspired by the belts and sashes that are an integral element of traditional Mayan costumes. The long, narrow shape of the piece reiterates the rectangular shape of the belts.

There are hundreds of different belts because each town uses distinctive colors, patterns and symbols. I've been collecting belts and sashes for more than two decades, and every piece in my collection is unique! Both men and women use them, and the men's belts are usually much wider than the women's.

The title "Chajul" [cha-hool] refers to a small town up in Guatemala's mountainous highlands. *Photo, Rolando Bianchi.*

22. "Nebaj"
35" x 55"

MATERIALS: Guatemalan hand-woven textiles and commercial cottons
TECHNIQUE: Machine pieced and quilted

Another design was inspired by the belts and sashes worn by the people of Nebaj ("nay-Bach"), a well-known town in Guatemala's mountainous highlands. The costume from Nebaj is one of the most regal and fine-looking in the country. The long, narrow shape of the piece reiterates the belts' rectangular shape.

I find diamonds irresistible, so they show up again and again in my work! I love their perfect geometric shape, their concentric "ripples" with infinite combination possibilities and the clean, diagonal lines they project. *Photo, Rolando Bianchi.*

23. "Whirlpools Going Round 'n Round"
(Remolinos dando Vueltas) 56" x 56"

MATERIALS: Guatemalan hand-woven textiles, Indonesian batiks and commercial cottons
TECHNIQUE: Paper pieced by machine and free-motion quilted

This piece is made up almost entirely of Guatemalan hand-woven textiles. It's a great example of how rich, colorful, textural, ethnic fabrics can create a very contemporary look. The carefully planned design takes into account the striped nature and Ikat quality of the Guatemalan fabrics, showing them off to their best advantage!

Movement starting within each of the nine small spirals continues around and into the middle and outer borders. Off-setting the panels reiterates the basic spiraling movement. Dashes of black and white reflect the "sparks" and help bring all the elements of the design together. *Photo, Rolando Bianchi.*

24. "Ferris Wheel"
(Rueda de Chicago) 57" x 57"

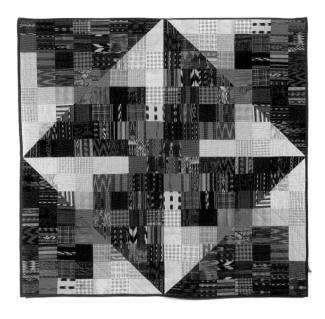

MATERIALS: Guatemalan hand-woven textiles and commercial plaids and cottons
TECHNIQUE: Machine pieced and quilted

This quilt is a study in value. I wanted to see if I could pull it off using Guatemalan fabrics almost exclusively. I discovered that the fabrics come in many bright medium and dark hues, but almost no light tones. I had to improvise and add most of the lights from U.S. plaids. It was a lucky mishap, because these two types of fabrics share the same rustic, simple, woven qualities and look great together!

There's an optical illusion of movement resulting from the careful placement of light and dark fabric patches. It is also a study in symmetry, since all four quarters are exactly the same; they were rotated to set the gigantic pinwheel design in motion. *Photo, Rolando Bianchi.*

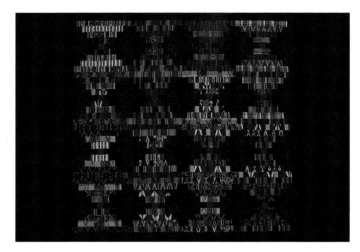

25. "Steps to Tikal"
(Gradas de Tikal) 56" x 56"

MATERIALS: Guatemalan hand-woven textiles and commercial cotton
TECHNIQUE: Machine pieced and quilted

Tikal is an ancient Mayan city hidden deep in the jungle of northern Guatemala's flatlands. A huge city by modern standards, it had many sky-high temples erected to worship the gods with thousands of steep steps. Playing around with the pieces on my design wall and seeing the way they decrease reminded me of those steps. The adaptation of a traditional "Courthouse Steps" block done in Guatemalan hand-wovens is an example of how two very different cultures can come together in a very successful way! *Photo, Rolando Bianchi.*

26. "Holy Week In Chichi"
(Semana Santa en Chichi) 30" x 30"

MATERIALS: Guatemalan hand-woven brocaded scrap of a "huipil" (Mayan woman's blouse) and commercial cottons
TECHNIQUE: Machine pieced and quilted

This Amish design came from "Little Book of Little Quilts" by Katharine Guerrier. I built the quilt around a scrap of a genuine Mayan woman's blouse to "Guatemalize" it. This "huipil" (we – peel) comes from the town of Chichicastenango ("Chichi" for short), known for its religious devotion. According to Catholic tradition, purple symbolizes the passion of Christ and thus is the color for Holy Week. The brocaded flowers harmonize with the familiar Amish color scheme.

In Guatemala, there are hundreds of different traditional costumes, each varying in style, colors and patterns. Each town or village has its own distinctive "traje," so you can identify where a person is from just by looking at how they're dressed. *Photo, Rolando Bianchi.*

From 2000 (Series II Continued):

"Art Quilts From Guatemalan Folklore"

Series II, an ongoing process of design highlighting ethnic fabrics, continued into 2000. The simple patterns displayed in this group of quilts lend themselves beautifully to the rich, colorful, rustic texture of my native Guatemalan hand-woven textiles. I continue to be challenged by the wide array of possibilities that the striped and nature of these textiles offer. *Photo, Rolando Bianchi.*

27. "Rain Forest"
(Bosque Tropical Húmedo) 36" x 49"

MATERIALS: Guatemalan hand-woven Indigos and textiles; gradated hand-dyed cottons
TECHNIQUE: Machine pieced and quilted

The urgent need to create this quilt came from a gradated assortment of hand-dyed fabrics that I just had to have!! They spoke to me (very clearly!) about green, lush vegetation, clear waterfalls and rain falling down. I chose a simple design that lets the rich Guatemalan textiles show off their beauty and pattern. Simplicity in design is all you need when working with such wonderful fabrics!

I love the exact, visually strong lines and the movement created by the clean, cool color scheme. Look at this quilt carefully, and you will hear the pouring rain and smell the wet earth below! Block inspired by Mary Mashuta's "Stripes in Quilts" book. *Photo, Rolando Bianchi.*

28. "Trip Around Toto"
(Viaje Alrededor de Totonicapán) 57" x 57"

MATERIALS: Guatemalan hand-woven textiles, Indonesian batiks and commercial cottons
TECHNIQUE: Machine pieced and free-motion quilted

This traditional Amish Sunshine & Shadow pattern, a.k.a Trip around the World, incorporates the unusual color scheme, texture and rustic beauty of hand-woven Mayan textiles. Most of the textiles were hand-woven by men on 36"-wide foot looms in a town called Totonicapán ("Toto" for short). This area in the highlands is one of Guatemala's major textile-producing Meccas. The endless variety of color combinations and patterns in our native textiles is due in part to the fact that each individual weaver has artistic license to create.

How two different cultures with substantial textile traditions can come together through my art quilts is very significant to me. *Photo, Rolando Bianchi. Quilted by Laura Lee Fritz.*

29. "Randa I"
47" x 47"

MATERIALS: Guatemalan hand-woven textiles and embroidered randas; commercial cottons

TECHNIQUE: Machine pieced and free-motion quilted

Randa is the heavily hand-embroidered decoration found on the front of native Mayan women's skirts. A single vertical line means the woman is single; married women wear a second horizontal line that crosses over and forms a cross shape.

The randa's linear nature inspired me to create this over-under woven design. The hot pink inner border holds everything together, while the blue-green hues provide a soothing background. Free-motion quilted flowers on the border reiterate the embroidered flowers in the central randa. *Photo, Rolando Bianchi. Quilted by Linda J. Stewart.*

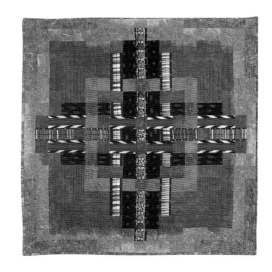

30. "Starbursts Go Red Hot"
(Estrellas Irradiando Calor) 39" x 50"

MATERIALS: Guatemalan hand-woven textiles, Indonesian batiks, commercial cottons; gradated hand-dyed border

TECHNIQUE: Machine pieced and quilted

This quilt began with a breathtaking hand-dyed fabric that gradated from yellow on one selvege through to purple on the other. This was going to be a wide border to showcase the fabric, and whatever I did in the center would have to change colors accordingly.

At the time I made this quilt, I challenged myself to stretch the possibilities of the stripes and designs frequently found on Guatemalan textiles. With this in mind, I chose a simple hexagon shape, fractured it, and cut the stripes so they would radiate into starbursts once the pieces were sewn back together. I love the synchronicity, richness and heat this quilt emanates. Each starburst falls perfectly into place! *Photo, Rolando Bianchi.*

31. "We Complement Each Other"
(Nos Complementamos Uno al Otro) 44" x 53"

MATERIALS: Guatemalan hand-woven, embroidered, and brocaded scraps of (assorted) Mayan women's blouses and commercial cottons

TECHNIQUE: Machine pieced and quilted

I thought I had won the lottery when I found these hand-woven heavily embroidered scraps at the craft market in Antigua. A man had a small basket overflowing with these multi-color squares, and I got them all! They are all different because they come from an assortment of huipiles. The strip-pieced block is from Kaffe Fassett's "Glorious Patchwork" book. *Photo, Rolando Bianchi.*

32. "Natura"
42½" x 56"

MATERIALS: Guatemalan hand-woven textiles, Indonesian batiks and commercial cottons
TECHNIQUE: Machine pieced and free-motion quilted

Guatemala has a tropical rain forest climate. Nature surrounds us with her impressive landscape and abundant, multi-colored flora and fauna, all of which influence our character. The colors in this quilt speak to us of the earth's green vegetation and the orange summery skies.

The richness and ethnic beauty of the hand-woven Guatemalan textiles add visual impact to this simple yet striking geometric design, inspired by Mary Mashuta's "Stripes in Quilts" book. I like to work with simple designs that let the rich native textiles show off! When working with such gorgeous fabric, just let the fabric lead the way. If you let go and listen to what it has to say, it'll take you places you never dreamed of! *Photo, Rolando Bianchi. Quilted by Laura Lee Fritz.*

33. "Giant Sunflower"
(Girasol Gigante) 58" x 80"

MATERIALS: Guatemalan hand-woven textiles, Indonesian batiks, African hand-stamped fabric and mud-cloth, commercial cottons
TECHNIQUE: Machine pieced, appliquéd and free-motion quilted

Creating this design was an interesting and extremely complicated process. In a class I took with Velda Newman, it started out as just a large flower head that I would hand-appliqué (yeah, sure!) onto a whole cloth background. I enjoyed hand-painting and shadowing the petals and center for a more realistic rendering, but other than that I was hopelessly stuck. A few years later, after taking a class from Ruth McDowell, a lightbulb lit up and the piece underwent major transformation! The stem and leaves were added, and the background was pieced using a multitude of patterns and textures. The exquisite mix of ethnic Guatemalan, Indonesian and African fabrics gives the bright, gorgeous flower a unique character. *Photo, Rolando Bianchi. Quilted by Laura Lee Fritz.*

34. "Stretched Diamond Star"
(Stella de Diamantes) 52" x 52"

MATERIALS: Guatemalan hand-woven textiles, gradated hand-dyed, commercial cottons and plaids
TECHNIQUE: Machine pieced and free-motion quilted

Although this quilt may look traditional, it is actually a new design in which a six-patch traditional square block has been literally s-t-r-e-t-c-h-e-d into a diamond-shaped wedge. The original Toad-in-the-Puddle block remains intact in the four background corners. I drafted a six-patch grid in the shape of a diamond and carefully transferred all the markings from the original block. This wedge forms the star.

To serve as the basis of my color scheme, I chose a packet of gradated hand-dyed fabric that included reddish brown, rusts and golden yellow. Then I added many more fabrics to the mix, following the basic color progression.

There's an air of mystery in this piece ... The symmetrical design captures attention while the luscious Guatemalan border fabric with its bargello-like motifs sets the mood. I like the deep, interesting center ending in a golden yellow aura and the outward movement the Star radiates. *Photo, Rolando Bianchi. Quilted by Linda J. Stewart.*

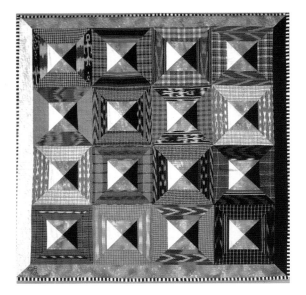

35. "Guatemalan Marble"
(Mármol de Guatemala) 34" x 43"

MATERIALS: Guatemalan hand-woven textiles, commercial cottons and plaids

TECHNIQUE: Machine pieced and free-motion quilted

I love the order and precision of geometric, repetitive patterns and have always been fascinated by European and Islamic mosaics and floor tile designs. This quilt, my second interpretation of Kaffe Fassett's Mosaic block, was inspired by antique tiles on the floor of St. Mark's Cathedral in Venice, Italy.

As usual, my goal was to incorporate Guatemalan textiles into the quilt. Each block is made of half hand-wovens and half plaids for a successful balance. The outer borders further emphasize the blocks' perspective. Although I don't usually work with only dark, serious colors, I found it soothing. Best of all, I really like the refined, elegant mood they project! *Photo, Rolando Bianchi.*

36. "The Stripes Made Me Do It"
(Las Rayas me Obligaron a Hacerlo) 34" x 43"

MATERIALS: Guatemalan hand-woven textiles, Indonesian batik and commercial cotton binding

TECHNIQUE: Machine pieced and quilted

This bold, simple geometric design creates optical illusions. These happen when the different stripes come together at an angle, creating squares within squares inside the blocks. Due to the weaving techniques used, many hand-woven Guatemalan fabrics have stripes. I'd estimate that of all the types of fabrics I use in my work, 80% are stripes — and I couldn't live without them!

Many styles of stripes went into this quilt. I used at least two different fabrics within the same square that don't match perfectly, and I'm not worried; even if they don't match, your eyes will make the connection! And the optical illusion will be there, playing now-you-see-it, now-you-don't tricks on the viewers. Working with stripes is a LOT of fun! *Photo, Rolando Bianchi.*

37. "Footpath to Todos Santos"
(Extravío a Todos Santos) 42½" x 55"

MATERIALS: Guatemalan hand-woven textiles, gradated hand-dyed and commercial cottons

TECHNIQUE: Machine pieced and free-motion quilted

Inspiration for this design came from traditional textiles worn by the people of Todos Santos in Guatemala's Mayan highlands. As tradition dictates, they use the vertical zigzag in their costume symbolizing the footpaths that people leave behind when walking up steep, frost-covered mountains. All of the vertical zigzags in this quilt came from only three hand-woven fabrics.

The gradated hand-dyed background that goes from fuchsia to lemon yellow glows with light and provides a fitting stage for the vertical zigzags. There's an interesting interplay of foreground and background in this design. There's movement as both jump out and recede at times —and symbiosis as they are inextricably connected.

This block was inspired by Mary Mashuta's "Stripes in Quilts" book. *Photo, Rolando Bianchi. Quilted by Laura Lee Fritz.*

38. "Nebaj II"
29½" x 55"

MATERIALS: Guatemalan hand-woven textiles and commercial cottons
TECHNIQUE: Machine pieced and quilted

This design was inspired by the bold, colorful diamonds on the belts worn by the people of Nebaj. The long, narrow shape of the piece reiterates the belts' rectangular shape. *Photo, Rolando Bianchi.*

From 2001 (Series III):

When I started quilting five years ago, I was aware that I was importing a completely foreign tradition into Guatemala. So, imprinting not only my own individual personality and style, but my Guatemalan identity as well, became of the utmost importance. I wanted to pay homage to my heritage, culture, Mayan influence and to traditional quilting.

39. "Randa II"
46½" x 48"

MATERIALS: Guatemalan hand-woven and embroidered randas, commercial cottons
TECHNIQUE: Machine pieced and quilted

Randa is the heavily hand-embroidered decoration holding together two selvedges or panels that butt against each other. The randa's linear nature inspired me to create this original, tessellating, woven lattice design. It represents the essence of weaving; the vertical randas being the warp while the horizontal wavy "threads" make up the weft. There is a never-ending feeling to a loom in its perpetual over-under motion. I see it as a symbol of perpetuating traditions.

I love the hot chili pepper red background — it makes a vibrant design! I used an array of black and white fabrics to tone it down and add a hint of drama! It took a lot of patience and partial seams to put this quilt together. It was very challenging but I'm very pleased with the results. *Photo, Pamela Cerezo.*

40. "Purple Cross"
(Cruz de Semana Santa) 46" x 52"

MATERIALS: Guatemalan hand-woven and embroidered textiles, Indonesian batiks and African and commercial cottons

TECHNIQUE: Machine pieced, appliquéd and free-motion quilted

This true scrap quilt was made with intuitive and spontaneous improvisational techniques only. If the block wasn't large enough, I'd add another piece; if it was too large, I'd cut off the excess. This was a relaxing and liberating creative process that I truly enjoyed. (Besides, I had to put to good use the zillions of scraps left over from so many previous quilts!)

We have a centuries-old Catholic tradition in Guatemala. Perhaps because I've lived in this environment all my life, the cross is a shape that I feel attracted to. It turns out in my compositions inadvertently — and I like it very much. It offers perfect balance and many "compartments" to work with.

The title refers to the color purple which, according to Catholic tradition, is used in Holy Week. *Photo, Pamela Cerezo. Quilted by Laura Lee Fritz.*

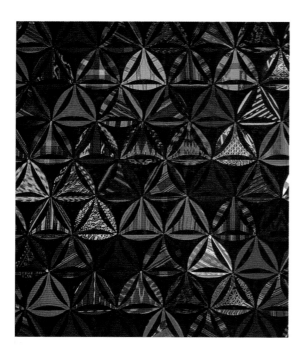

41. "Rainbow Oranges"
(Arcoiris de Naranjas) 55" x 59"

MATERIALS: Guatemalan hand-woven textiles and commercial cottons

TECHNIQUE: Machine pieced and free-motion quilted

I used a traditional Orange Peel design with a twist, since the repeat block unit is a triangular shape instead of the usual square. Multicolor Guatemalan fabrics were used over a dark navy background to create contrast and drama. The dark background recedes, letting the multicolor triangles advance and show to full advantage.

This design is based on "Notan," the Eastern principle that concentrates on the interaction between positive (or shape) and negative (or background) space. If you look closely, you'll notice that there's a negative (dark navy) triangle for each positive (multicolor) one. The negative space is equally important, for it "saves the space" for the positive figure to work successfully. *Photo, Pamela Cerezo. Quilted by Beverly Rodgers.*

42. "December 7th"
(La Quema del Diablo) 56" x 56"

MATERIALS: Guatemalan hand-woven solid textiles, Indonesian batiks, hand-dyes and commercial cottons

TECHNIQUE: Machine pieced and free-motion quilted kaleidoscope design

Every year on December 7th, Guatemalans celebrate a semi-religious, folkloric festivity called "the Burning of the Devil." All over the country, huge bonfires are lit and devil-like piñatas and figures are burnt to cleanse our spirits from evil. Notice how the design incorporates elements and representations of fire, heat, ashes and flames.

I began creating this quilt with a completely different idea in mind — it was going to be a black white white, mandala-type piece. But it soon became boring, and working intuitively as I do, I let the fabric take it from there. I like the wholeness of the symmetrical design and the flame-like warm-colored border. *Photo, Pamela Cerezo. Quilted by Beverly Rodgers*

43. "El Kite-O"
(El Barrilete) 46" x 50"

MATERIALS: Guatemalan hand-woven textiles, Indonesian batiks and commercial cottons

TECHNIQUE: Machine pieced and free-motion quilted

Kites are very much a part of our indigenous Mayan traditions. Every year on November 1st, the "Day of the Dead," people go to the cemeteries by the thousands. They pay their respects to relatives and friends who have passed away, and huge multicolor paper-and-bamboo kites, which measure up to 20 feet across, are elevated from many cemetery grounds to carry the souls of the dead to Heaven. It's breathtaking to see hundreds of them filling up the sky! Kites are a recurring theme in my work. I love their shape, colors, patterns and especially their symbolism.

I jokingly entitled this "El Kite-O," because English speakers think that if you add an "o" to the end of a word, you're speaking Spanish! *Photo, Pamela Cerezo. Quilted by Beverly Rodgers.*

44. "Sunset At The Beach"
(Atardecer en la Playa) 50½" x 65"

MATERIALS: Guatemalan hand-woven textiles, gradated hand-dyes and commercial cottons

TECHNIQUE: Machine pieced and free-motion quilted

This quilt resembles the sun setting on the horizon (golds and yellows) on a beautiful, deep-colored late afternoon sky (top purples) over water (center turquoise patches). With a little imagination, the bottom greens could even be mountains! I love the tranquil feeling this piece gives of images being reflected on water.

This original tessellating design was challenging to make, and I had a hard time understanding how it worked until I was putting it together. I was inspired by an old children's craft book on cutting and folding back paper. *Photo, Pamela Cerezo. Quilted by Beverly Rodgers.*

45. "Guatemalan Blocks"
(Trozos Guatemaltecos) 70" x 77"

MATERIALS: Guatemalan hand-woven textiles, U.S. commercial cottons and plaids

TECHNIQUE: Machine pieced and free-motion quilted

This quilt was acquired by New York City's Museum of Arts & Design (former American Craft Museum) in April 2002, three years after I first started exhibiting my work in public. It became part of their Permanent Collection, which they describe as a "showcase of the best contemporary art quilts from around the world." There are 50 pieces in the collection, and I'm the only Central American artist represented.

"Guatemalan Blocks" has traveled worldwide as part of the Museum's "Six Continents of Quilts" exhibit. The Museum chose it as a testament to how the American art of quilting has spread around the world. Furthermore, it symbolizes a fusion of two great textile cultures: a traditional, purely American Baby Blocks pattern done with non-traditional Guatemalan hand-woven textiles.

The careful placement of light, medium and dark fabric patches gives a dramatic look and creates an optical illusion of volume. It is amazing to see how a flat surface can give so much depth and perspective! *Photo, Pamela Cerezo. Quilted by Beverly Rodgers.*

46. "Sunset: Fractured Landscape"

(Celajes en la Costa) 45" x 37"

MATERIALS: Indonesian batiks and commercial cottons

TECHNIQUE: Machine pieced, appliquéd and free-motion quilted

When I saw a magnificent photograph, I was smitten! The wonderful tree reminds me of my childhood — living at the farm on Guatemala's Pacific coast, we'd watch the hot summer afternoon sky with orange and fiery red nuances.

The fractured surface is a great excuse to use more fabric! The design is from nature, inspired by techniques in "Fractured Landscapes," by Katie Pasquini Masopust. *Photo, Pamela Cerezo. Original photo by David Lorenz Winston, http://www.david-lorenzwinston.com/. Quilted by Laura Lee Fritz.*

From 2002 (Series IV):

Using my native fabric has gradually changed my style toward something more of my own, strengthening the direct influence of my roots and the cultural context that I live in. My style has become more liberated! When people see my art quilts, they will see a colorful, bright Guatemala reflected under a positive, new light.

47. "Blooming Natura II"

(Natura Florida II) 42½" x 56½"

MATERIALS: Guatemalan hand-woven textiles, Indonesian batiks and commercial cottons

TECHNIQUE: Machine pieced and free-motion quilted

The colors in this quilt flow and transform as they blend with each other, with the help of "transition" fabrics. They represent the abundant, tropical Guatemalan flora.

I always view my art quilts as "one surface" (like a painter sees the canvas), and not as so many blocks across, so many blocks down. In other words, I try not to see each block as separate, but as a contributing part to the whole. So in this quilt, although the geometric design is based on a repetitive grid, no two blocks are alike due to the unique way in which fabrics are applied. This quilt was inspired by "Stripes in Quilts," by Mary Mashuta. *Photo, Alan Benchoam. Quilted by Laura Lee Fritz.*

48. "RhapSSSody"
(RapSSSodia) 36½" x 67½"

MATERIALS: Guatemalan hand-woven textiles, Indonesian batiks, African mud-cloth and commercial cottons

TECHNIQUE: Innovative, free-form cutting techniques; machine pieced and free-motion quilted

I was experimenting with improvisational cutting and sewing techniques, which resulted in a spur-of-the-moment kind of creative process. Although I work intuitively and quite fast, I do measure accurately and use templates to get precise results. So, piling up a bunch of squares and just cutting them free-hand is not my cup of tea. However, I must confess that I enjoyed this spontaneous process tremendously! It was fun, relaxing and liberating, and I love how the "S" curves give movement and rhythm to this bold, asymmetrical, contemporary design. *Photo, Alan Benchoam. Quilted by Laura Lee Fritz*

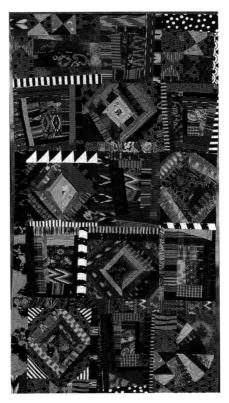

49. "A Square is A Square, is A Square"
(Cuadros, Cuadros y Más Cuadros) 57½" x 60"

MATERIALS: Guatemalan hand-woven textiles, Indonesian batiks and commercial cottons

TECHNIQUE: Machine pieced and free-motion quilted

I like the orderliness and precision of how squares fit together in this modern, geometric design. It's a simple idea that's been repeated many times; four triangles making up a square. Adding variety in scale (different sizes) infuses the quilt with energy and vibrancy!

What began as a blue-and-white-only idea soon developed into a richer, heartier color scheme with the addition of neighboring colors like turquoise, purple and fuchsia. The idea came from "Passionate Patchwork," by Kaffe Fassett.

Photo, Alan Benchoam. Quilted by Laura Lee Fritz.

50. "Multicolored Sash"
(Faja Multicolor) 33½" x 63"

MATERIALS: Guatemalan hand-woven, embroidered and brocaded textiles, Indonesian batiks, hand-dyed and commercial cottons

TECHNIQUE: Improvisational, free-form cutting techniques; machine pieced and free-motion quilted

This contemporary scrap quilt resulted from an intuitive, exciting and creative process of improvisational techniques. I included traditional blocks (Hourglass and Granny's Fan), but cut them free-hand to look catawampus and in sync with the mood of the piece. The asymmetrical composition in bright, multi-colors inspires a happy, festive mood. This piece has the spontaneity and simplicity of African-American quilts, which is one of my favorite styles.

The design represents the sashes and belts that are an essential part of Mayan men and women's costumes. It has assorted elements taken from the costumes of several different towns. *Photo, Alan Benchoam. Quilted by Laura Lee Fritz.*

51. "Holiday in Nebaj (IV)"

(Nebaj en Fiesta IV) 40½" x 41"

MATERIALS: Guatemalan hand-woven textiles, Indonesian batiks and commercial cottons

TECHNIQUE: Machine pieced and quilted

Multi-colored, never-ending geometric designs made of striped fabric triangles were carefully placed together to form larger squares. The resulting sub-patterns along the seam-lines create the optical illusion of squares-within-squares. Some areas recede while others advance; deep, dark colors give depth, and diamonds seem to appear and disappear.

Inspiration for this visually rich piece came from the tessellating shapes on the traditional belt worn by the people of Nebaj. I love how the attractive Guatemalan fabrics show their character! *Photo, Alan Benchoam.*

52. "Serpentines"

(Serpentinas) 60" x 70"

MATERIALS: Guatemalan hand-woven textiles and commercial cottons

TECHNIQUE: Machine pieced and free-motion quilted

Every now and then, my fingers itch to sew curves. I'm attracted to the winding forms created by the Snake Trail block, and the eye-catching color combination is a winner! It was inspired by our fuchsia and Chinese red kitchen from when I was a teenager in the' 70s. The daring warm hues are lighter toward the center and darkest around the edges to suggest a border. *Photo, Alan Benchoam. Quilted by Laura Lee Fritz.*

53. "Confetti in San Pedro"

(Confeti en San Pedro) 50" x 53"

MATERIALS: Guatemalan hand-woven textiles and heavily hand-embroidered skirt decoration called "randa", commercial cottons

TECHNIQUE: Machine pieced and free-motion quilted

When visiting San Pedro Sacatepéquez, a large town close to Guatemala City, I stood in awe admiring the tapestry of hourglasses and diamonds on a Mayan woman's huipil. I just had to incorporate this idea into a quilt, and my geometric rendering is based on the Hourglass block, of course!

The assortment of bright colors contrasts with the crispness of the black and white dashes. It's interesting to see how the horizontal central areas of gradated warm and cool colors bring all the elements of the design together in harmony. *Photo, Alan Benchoam. Quilted by Beverly Rodgers.*

54. "Lake Atitlan"
(Lago de Atitlán) 73" x 48½"

MATERIALS: Guatemalan hand-woven textiles, Indonesian batiks, African mud-cloth, hand-dyed and commercial cottons

TECHNIQUE: Machine pieced, appliquéd and free-motion quilted using Sashiko patterns.

I've been inspired my whole life to create this landscape quilt. Lake Atitlan is a must-visit landmark in the highlands, and many consider it to be the most beautiful lake in the world. I've visited many, many times, and every time it takes my breath away!

I chose appropriate fabrics that would depict the distinct elements: sky, water, mountains, volcanoes, corn field, vegetation and earth. I added borders that would reiterate the elements they surround and remind us of the origins of art quilting. *Photo, Pamela Cerezo. Quilted by Beverly Rodgers. Original photograph by Marino Cattelan.*

55. "Giant Kite With Shadow"
(Barrilete Gigante con Sombra) 56" x 68½"

MATERIALS: Guatemalan hand-woven textiles, Indonesian batiks, hand-dyes, African and commercial cottons

TECHNIQUE: Machine pieced and free-motion quilted

Kites are very much a part of our indigenous Mayan traditions. Every year on November 1st, we celebrate the "Day of the Dead," and beautifully decorated huge kites fly from the cemeteries.

A great deal of realism has been achieved in this off-center design. The huge size of the quilt mimics the size of the actual tissue paper and bamboo kites, and the concentric circles were done with solid cottons. The dark border was pieced in a darker shade of each color to create the "shadow" effect. This was very challenging to make — I had to sew all of the pieces with extra care to keep the border line perfectly aligned, or the visual effect would have been ruined. *Photo, Alan Benchoam. Quilted by Beverly Rodgers.*

56. "Reflections"
(Reflejos) 49" x 60"

MATERIALS: Scraps of Guatemalan hand-woven textiles, Indonesian batiks, hand-dyes and commercial cottons

TECHNIQUE: String-pieced by machine and free-motion quilted

True scrap quilting uses improvisational techniques where the spontaneous, creative process is the main focus. Hundreds of horizontal strips that connect and break — only to connect again — create movement and give the impression of a mirage reflecting sky over water. The rich, complementary color scheme is striking!

At the time I made this quilt, I had tons of leftover scraps and I wanted to try out different ideas. I started putting together the most unusual and unexpected fabric strips into sets. (It was a pleasant surprise later on when I realized how rich this mix made the quilt look!) Not really knowing where to go from there, I cut big triangles, put together diamonds, and created a frame with analogous (violet) setting triangles. The whole thing was an enjoyable intuitive process! *Photo, Carina Woolrich. Quilted by Laura Lee Fritz.*

From 2003 (Series V):

I showcase what's being done in art quilting in Latin America and share the inter-cultural and ethnic qualities of my work with international audiences. This work is inspired by specific Mayan textiles — focusing on blouses, belts and skirts — to create one-of-a-kind contemporary pieces. This series of art quilts has been a raving success! It's been exhibited internationally and published extensively.

57. "Nebaj III"
38" x 57"

MATERIALS: Guatemalan hand-woven textiles, Indonesian ba-tiks and commercial cottons

TECHNIQUE: Machine pieced and free-motion quilted

The costume from Nebaj is perhaps the most spectacular and attractive of all Mayan costumes. This design is my contempo-rary interpretation of the shapes found on the belt. Multi-colored diamonds are definitely one of my favorite geometric designs, and they show up again and again in my artwork. Here, I have splurged and enjoyed creating many variations. Repeating the basic diamond shape gives unity to the array of forms and colors.
Photo, Alan Benchoam. Quilted by Laura Lee Fritz.

58. "Ceremony In Patzún"
(Ceremonia en Patzún) 45" x 51"

MATERIALS: Guatemalan hand-woven textiles, Indonesian batiks and commercial cottons

TECHNIQUE: Machine pieced and free-motion quilted

Brides from Patzún [pat-zoon] proudly wear a "paya" or head-dress on their wedding day. This ceremonial cloth of pre-Hispanic origin is brimming with symbols which will protect and provide the newlyweds with good fortune.

In my interpretation, the central diamond symbolizes the sun as the center of the universe; the top and bottom cir-cles are the stages of the moon; the central zigzagging mo-tifs are the nine months of pregnancy and fertility; and the overall hourglass design represents the duality of life (yin and yang; man and woman; good and evil; night and day), all coming together in harmony. The multi-colored border reminds me of the Guatemalan rainbow. *Photo, Alan Benchoam. Quilted by Laura Lee Fritz.*

59. "Furrows of Almolonga"
(Sembradíos de Almolonga) 64" x 60"

MATERIALS: Guatemalan hand-woven textiles, Indonesian batiks, African prints, hand-dyed and commercial cottons
TECHNIQUE: Machine pieced and free-motion quilted

Almolonga provides the Central American countries with fresh vegetables all year long. It's a thriving agricultural community located on a fertile valley, blessed with many water springs. The land's influence on its people is so profound that they have woven this reality for posterity into their costumes and textiles. The furrows on the land become zigzags on the cloth. A sudden break on the weaving pattern resembles folds on the field that interrupt the uniform rows of vegetables. *Photo, Alan Benchoam. Quilted by Laura Lee Fritz.*

60. "Colors of San Ildefonso"
(Colores de San Ildefonso) 46" x 71"

MATERIALS: Guatemalan hand-woven textiles and commercial cottons
TECHNIQUE: Machine pieced and free-motion quilted

I was irresistibly attracted to the neatly organized X shapes on the huipil of a woman from San Ildefonso. My creative juices were flowing as I started by isolating one motif and changing its scale. Then, I picked out the colors from the blouse and skirt themselves, and arranged them in a pleasant analogous palette. I love the graphic appeal and methodical style of this piece. *Photo, Alan Benchoam. Quilted by Laura Lee Fritz.*

61. "The Collar of San Cristóbal Toto"
(El Huipil de San Cristóbal Totonicapán) 50" x 48"

MATERIALS: Guatemalan hand-woven, hand-dyed and embroidered textiles, Indonesian batiks and commercial cottons
TECHNIQUE: Machine pieced, appliquéd and free-motion quilted

The costume from San Cristóbal Totonicapán ("Toto" for short) has a strong Spanish influence. The traditional huipil, with its heavily embroidered collar and scalloped, lacy borders, is reminiscent of 17th Century Spanish costumes. These details contributed to the blouse's festive mood and denoted its character as a symbol of heritage and wealth.

I enjoyed adding a variety of flowers and shapes when re-interpreting this design. I love its asymmetric balance, the contrast between circular and square shapes, and the magnificent hand-dyed whole cloth background. This quilt has a happy spirit! *Photo, Alan Benchoam. Quilted by Beverly Rodgers.*

62. "Chichi's Cross"
(Cruz de Chichi) 47" x 47"

MATERIALS: Guatemalan hand-woven textiles, Indonesian batiks and commercial cottons

TECHNIQUE: Machine pieced and free-motion quilted

This design symbolizes the community of Chichicastenango united around the sign of the cross. "Chichi" (for short) is well known as a main religious site in Guatemala, deeply devoted to both their Catholic and indigenous beliefs.

These are the colors that can be appreciated in many of Chichi's textiles and huipiles. The center of the blouse that goes over the head displays a radial motif suggestive of the sun as the center of the universe, as well as masculine power. The four diamonds symbolize the phases of the moon and feminine power.

I love the contrast achieved between the intricately detailed kaleidoscopic center and the simple, large areas of deep color around it.
Photo, Alan Benchoam. Quilted by Beverly Rodgers.

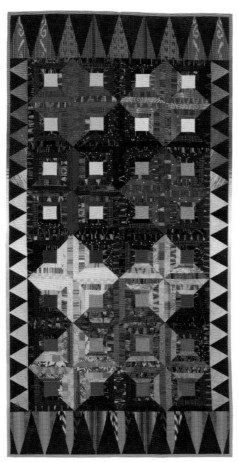

63. "Tapestry from Aguas Calientes"
(Tapiz de Aguas Calientes) 67" x 55"

MATERIALS: Guatemalan hand-woven textiles, randas and commercial cottons

TECHNIQUE: Machine pieced, appliquéd and free-motion quilted

The women from Aguas Calientes, a town just outside the colonial city of Antigua, are renowned for weaving the finest brocade in the country. The tiny, detailed overall pattern of an unusual huipil spoke to me directly and guided my inspiration. For this original design, I chose an Amish color palette to achieve a more formal look — Guatemalan textiles and Amish colors complement each other in the best way! I enjoyed adding the central horizontal and vertical strips to symbolize the center seam and shoulder division of the unfolded huipil. *Photo, Alan Benchoam. Quilted by Laura Lee Fritz.*

64. "Log Cabin Sash"
(Faja de Cruces) 34½" x 70"

MATERIALS: Guatemalan hand-woven textiles, Indonesian batiks and commercial cottons

TECHNIQUE: Machine pieced, appliquéd and free-motion quilted

I enjoy taking a conventional quilting block and giving it a twist to "Guatemalize" it; it's my way of paying homage to tradition. Inspired by the belts worn by the people of San Juan Sacatepéquez, I decided to use Log Cabins in a different context, giving them a totally altered look. Instead of the usual light-dark setting, two bright colors (green-brown) were placed side-by-side. I like the big color chunks that result, and I love how the centers of four adjacent blocks "frame" each cross. The triangle border further emphasizes the color scheme and replicates the fringe from the belts. I love to create movement through the transition of colors changing into one another.

Dark navy is the perfect background to make the fabric pop, and the multi-color crosses really jump out out at you! *Photo, Alan Benchoam. Quilted by Laura Lee Fritz.*

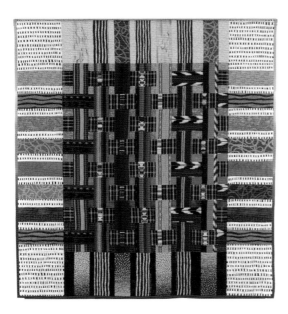

65. "Mayan Kente (Randa III)"

50" x 56"

MATERIALS: Guatemalan hand-woven textiles, hand-embroidered "randas," hand-dyed and commercial cottons

TECHNIQUE: Machine pieced and free-motion quilted

I've long been attracted to randas. They display different shapes like flowers, jugs, pitchers and geometric figures, and their linear nature suggested "weaving" to me. The continuous motion of weft over and under warp is the fundamental essence of textiles. As I worked the design, it reminded me of Kente cloth from Africa. The weaving process, its fundamental nature, and its looks are all very similar. I raise my hat to all cloth weavers, thanking them for the legacy left behind for us to enjoy. *Photo, Alan Benchoam. Quilted by Laura Lee Fritz.*

66. "Sunshine and Shadows in San Juan"

(Sol y Sombra en San Juan) 56" x 56"

MATERIALS: Guatemalan hand-woven textiles, Indonesian batiks and commercial cottons

TECHNIQUE: Machine pieced and free-motion quilted

I was in the mood to sew some curves, so I was searching through an old book for ideas. Inspiration hit when I came upon this Sunshine & Shadows pattern (a traditional 4x4 setting of Drunkard's Path blocks from the 1930s, attributed to Carlie Sexton). I liked the vibrant, unusual way of putting the blocks together. Since I only wanted to use two or three bright, bold colors, I applied the color scheme from the costume of San Juan Sacatepéquez. What a perfect combination! I further "Guatemalized" the design by piecing a diamond of striped hand-woven textiles in the middle of each center block. *Quilted by Laura Lee Fritz.*

67. "Rainbow Forest"

(Bosque Arcoiris) 36" x 49"

MATERIALS: Guatemalan hand-woven textiles and commercial cottons

TECHNIQUE: Machine pieced and free-motion quilted

I'm strongly attracted to the zigzag motif for its dynamic nature and visual movement. Having created this design before, I wanted to experiment with a different color palette. When my purpose to let the rich Guatemalan textiles show off their beauty and texture was revealed, all the colors of the rainbow wanted in on it! All of that intense color called for a muted background, and that's how the black-to-gray-to-white gradation came about.

I like the high contrast between bright foreground and tranquil background; the interplay of center background and self-border is clever, and polka dots add a touch of whimsy! The block was inspired by "Stripes in Quilts," by Mary Mashuta. *Quilted by Christine's Custom Quilts.*

Special Quilts:

The following three quilts were made with a special purpose in mind. They are not my usual art quilts, because they had to conform to certain specifications to showcase my fabric line for Robert Kaufman, to demo on a show or to teach a specific class.

68. "Colors of San Antonio"

(Colores de San Antonio) 66" x 44"

MATERIALS: U.S. commercial cottons from my collection "Guatemalan Rainbow" for Robert Kaufman Fabrics, October 2004

TECHNIQUE: Machine pieced and free-motion quilted

I created this quilt to showcase my first fabric collection inspired by Guatemalan time-honored textiles! I chose the traditional Snowball block because it has a large central area to display the fabric in large chunks. I love geometric shapes and happy, multi-colored designs!

The repetitive blocks are like a magnified version of stitches and patterns woven into the huipiles of San Antonio Aguas Calientes, a well-known textile "Mecca." This quilt was featured in "Quiltmaker" magazine's Sept/Oct '05 #105 issue. *Quilted by Peg Spradlin.*

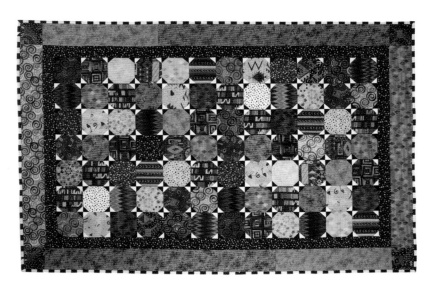

69. "Mayan Rainbow"

(Arcoiris Maya) May 2003 66" x 78"

MATERIALS: Guatemalan hand-woven textiles and commercial cottons

TECHNIQUE: Machine pieced and free-motion quilted

I created this quilt to be featured on "Quilt Central" TV Show on PBS. I was asked to re-decorate an entire bedroom with my quilts, and this was the centerpiece ("Guatemalan Bedroom" Episode 409, Series 400). The "Courthouse Steps" block gave lots of space to showcase as many hand-woven fabrics as I wanted. I cut up a 2½" strip out of every single fabric in my Guatemalan stash, in every color! (Scraps would be fantastic too!)

In a design such as this, the positive space (multi-colored blocks) is as important as the negative (background). The background gives the blocks room to breathe, so the overall effect is balanced and visually pleasing. Without the negative space, the color and pattern variety would be overpowering and displeasing. I often choose a dark navy or navy-black background fabric to achieve high contrast.

This quilt was also featured in the summer 2004 issue of the premiere French magazine "Quiltmania." *Photo, Guy Yoyotte-Husson. Quilted by Tina Collins.*

70. "Glowing Stars"
(Estrellas Radiantes) July 2004 52½" x 57"

MATERIALS: Guatemalan hand-woven textiles and commercial cottons
TECHNIQUE: Machine pieced and free-motion quilted

While teaching classes around the world, I discovered that quilters could not necessarily dive right into a complicated quilt bursting with color. I needed to begin with a familiar, traditional block that would take students by the hand and bring them out of their comfort zones smoothly.

This star quilt is what I created for that purpose. It's made from half Guatemalan fabrics (the stars), and half U.S. commercial cottons, all from the same collection (the backgrounds). Students have used African, Australian aboriginal and South African Dutch prints, Indonesian batiks, Japanese yukatas and even Indian silks! No matter what fabrics they choose, the result is always stunning! *Quilted by Christine's Custom Quilts.*

From 2005 (Series VI):

In the summer of 2004, I traveled to teach at South Africa's National Quilt Festival. This was a life-changing experience! Africa made a lasting impression on me and the wonderful, warm people I met stole my heart.

Ethnic motifs in arts and crafts from around the world have always attracted me because of their similarity with Guatemalan cultural expressions. The ethnic qualities of my work have always mirrored the culturally diverse context I live in. After experiencing Africa for myself, I know that it would have a strong influence on my future work.

The following art quilts premiered during my solo show at the National Museum of Modern Art "Carlos Mérida" in Guatemala City, April 2006.

---

71. "African Cross"
(Cruz Africana) 48" x 69"

MATERIALS: Guatemalan hand-woven textiles, Indonesian batiks, commercial and hand-dyed cottons
TECHNIQUE: Machine pieced and free-motion quilted with Kachina-style designs

It took me about two years to complete this quilt. A while back, I had wanted to experiment with improvisational techniques like free-form rotary cutting. I ended up with kind-of-crooked-looking blocks that I didn't really like much. At the time I was working with precise, straight geometric lines, and these really didn't fit into anything I was doing. So, I stored them away and forgot about them for more than two years — until I went to Africa.

I was so inspired by everything I saw and experienced in South Africa that I needed to make a special quilt to express everything I felt. The improvisational blocks from a couple of years ago were exactly what I needed to begin! I sketched away during the flight home; the ideas were flowing, and I couldn't wait to get back into my studio.

As if they knew their place, the central blocks fell effortlessly into a cross shape. Because they seemed too similar I decided to use an unexpected, contrasting palette for the four corner areas of the quilt. I love how it adds depth to the background and makes the central cross stand out! The yellow and white checkerboards add sparkle.

Photo, Alan Benchoam. Quilted by Laura Lee Fritz.

72. "African Roots"
(Raíces Africanas) 62" x 63"

MATERIALS: Guatemalan hand-woven textiles, commercial cottons and hand-dyed background
TECHNIQUE: Machine pieced and free-motion quilted

From my trip to South Africa, I brought home a gorgeous African shirt with cross motifs over a monochromatic gray background. I had also bought a breathtaking length of hand-dyed fabric with a weird color combination that grabbed me (red wine, raspberry, mustard yellow and pastel mint green). At dawn one morning, I woke up with a crystal clear idea of how I could combine the two elements into one quilt design! Soon, I started auditioning Guatemalan textiles for the crosses. I love how the background made me choose unusual color combinations.

Notice how the four left columns are positive while the two right columns are negative. *Photo, Alan Benchoam. Quilted by Laura Lee Fritz.*

73. "African Roots, Part II"
(Raíces Africanas, Parte II) 45" x 45½"

74. "African Roots, The Trilogy"
(Raíces Africanas, La Trilogía) 34½" x 34½"

MATERIALS: Guatemalan hand-woven textiles, Indonesian batiks, commercial and hand-dyed cottons
TECHNIQUE: Machine pieced and free-motion quilted

These two quilts happened by accident. I was ironing a chain of sashing squares for the first "African Roots," when wham! It hit me — these squares look great on their own. What if I made another quilt with basically the same color scheme, using only smaller squares and leaving out the crosses? Bam! Part II was born. I added sashing for a more formal look (and because I couldn't have enough of that divine South African hand-dye!).

For "The Trilogy," I restrained from sashing and left the squares alone. I love the modernistic feel to these pieces and the areas of light and dark that yield optical illusions. *Photos, Alan Benchoam. Quilted by Laura Lee Fritz.*

75. "Warm Day in Nebaj (V)"
(Día Cálido en Nebaj V) 31½" x 50"

76. "Cool Night in Nebaj (VI)"
(Noche Fría en Nebaj VI) 31½" x 50"

MATERIALS: Guatemalan hand-woven textiles, Indonesian batiks and commercial cottons

TECHNIQUE: Machine pieced and free-motion quilted

These are renderings V and VI of an ongoing quilt series based on one of my favorite geometric shapes. These quilts were inspired by diamonds portrayed on the wide belts worn daily by the people of Nebaj. Women wear an elaborate wrapped headdress with tassels, a huipil with brocaded human, animal and triangular bird motifs, a red skirt and a striped shawl. Geometric shapes are ever-present in Mayan textiles; in this case, the belt has diamonds enclosing double triangles.

Women weave their own clothes on backstrap looms. They may wear only one or two huipils throughout their lifetime, which is why they're practical and made to last. "Warm Day" refers to a warm color scheme; "Cool Night" uses a cool color scheme. *Photos, Alan Benchoam. Quilted by Laura Lee Fritz.*

76. "Eye Candy"
(Rosario de Dulces) 40½" x 60"

MATERIALS: Guatemalan hand-woven textiles, Indonesian batiks and commercial cottons

TECHNIQUE: Machine pieced and free-motion quilted

Working with the colors and shapes in this quilt suddenly brought back a childhood memory. On Sunday afternoons, my parents would take my brothers and me for a drive around Lake Amatitlán, and we'd stop at the park on the waterfront to buy sweets from local vendors in their stands brimming with goodies. My favorites were the sugar candy rosaries, multi-colored raffia tied-up in the shape of beads that formed a closed loop like a rosary. It was exciting to open each bead-like pouch to find the hidden candy within. We'd wear the rosaries like a necklace, hang them from our bed posts and scoop out candy for days! *Photo, Alan Benchoam. Quilted by Laura Lee Fritz.*

78. "Aguacatán"
36" x 37"

MATERIALS: Stripes from Guatemalan hand-woven textiles, Indonesian batiks and commercial cottons

TECHNIQUE: Machine pieced and free-motion quilted

After driving for endless hours along meandering dirt roads, one arrives at the agricultural town of Aguacatán [ε-wa-ca-tan], whose name derives from the local "aguacate" (avocaco) trees. Located in western Guatemala at the foot of the Cuchumatanes Mountains, this town enjoys a warm climate.

Women here wear a rather simple white muslin huipil with machine embroidery decorations banded with tucks and colored ribbons. In contrast, they weave and wear an elaborate and sophisticated headdress. It consists of a 4"-wide, 3 yd.-long ribbon, painstakingly brocaded with an infinite variety of geometric and sometimes organic motifs (like leaves), that they braid and wrap around their heads.

This quilt shows one of the triangular motifs from Aguacatan's head ribbon done in a way that creates optical illusions. *Photo, Alan Benchoam. Quilted by Laura Lee Fritz.*

Glossary of Mayan Textile Terms

Capixay

Garment of European origin worn by indigenous men from the highlands. It is a type of wool tunic with an opening in the middle for the head. It sometimes has false sleeves that fall to the side or that are incorporated into the garment. The name is likely derived from the Basque capusayo or kapusay.

Cofradía

Religious brotherhood dedicated to the veneration of a particular saint or charitable work. Introduced by the Catholic Church during the Colonial period as a means of spreading the faith. Its development, like that of other social institutions, is characterized by a process of syncretism through which European and indigenous cultural elements were fused. Its members wear distinctive garments, which denote their office, social status and rank.

Corte

Called uk' in the Mayan languages, indigenous women wear their skirts either wrapped or pleated. The wrapped skirt is of pre-Hispanic origin and the pleated skirt shows European influence. In some communities, the skirts vary in color, decorative figures and the way they are worn. Nowadays, however, many villages are using a regional-style skirt that is made in the ikat (tie-dye) technique.

Faja

With very few exceptions, women use sashes to hold up their skirts. Most sashes are woven on the backstrap loom. In some villages sashes differ in width; the older or mature women wear belts that are wider than the ones young women wear. When indigenous men adopt western clothing, the piece they tend to conserve is the woven sash.

Huipil

The huipil is used by the indigenous women of Guatemala to cover their torso. Its use dates back to pre-Hispanic times. It can be woven on a backstrap loom or foot loom or it can be made of commercial material; it may be embroidered by hand or machine. Generally the huipil is the most colorful part of the Mayan costume. Each community's weaving has distinctive characteristics such as color, decorative figures, number of panels, and the techniques used in its creation. Nowadays, however, towns often influence one another.

Perraje or shawl

A perraje or tapado is a shawl which may be worn by indigenous women over their shoulders, to cover their heads, or folded over their arm or head. It is also used for carrying small children on their back. It is of European origin and it's woven mostly on foot looms. It may be finished with knots, fringe or tassels.

Ponchito

Fringed rectangular wool cloth with weft stripes; or warp and weft designs forming a black and white checkerboard pattern; it may be embroidered. Indigenous men from different communities may wear them only in front, at waist level, over their trousers or like an apron. It is held in place by a belt or sash.

Rodillera

Rectangular wool cloth with warp and weft designs forming a brown and white checkerboard pattern. Wrapped around the hips by indigenous men from Sololá, San Antonio Palopó and Nahualá, and held in place by a belt or sash. Depending on the town's custom, short or long trousers are worn underneath.

Su't or cloth

The su't is a large, square cloth that has several uses: to transport and wrap children, to carry merchandise, to protect the wearer from the sun, to cover the head, arms or shoulders on ceremonial occasions, and to hold ritual objects or sacred images. Its size and type of decoration may vary according to the textile tradition of each community and how it is used.

Tocado or head-dress

Indigenous women from many villages are accustomed to complement their dress with distinctive head ornaments. These can be divided into cintas and tocoyales. Cintas are ribbons or bands of cloth, woven in cotton, wool, silk, rayon or acrylic fibers, and vary a great deal in size, material, decoration and the form in which they are worn. Tocoyales are wool cords.

Traje or full dress

The generic term traje refers to the full traditional Mayan dress or costume that identifies the wearer's origin or her/his ethnicity, be it man or woman. It is used to describe everyday clothing as well as ceremonial garments.

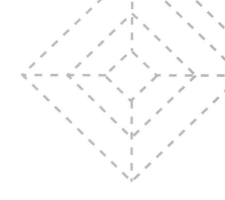

Recommended Bibliography

"5000 Years of Textiles"
Edited by Jennifer Harris
British Museum Press, London, 1993

"African Designs from
Traditional Sources"
by Geoffrey Williams
Dover Publications, Inc.,
Minneola, NY, 1971

"American Indian Design & Decoration"
by Leroy H. Appleton
Dover Publications, Inc.,
New York, NY, 1950, 1971

"Charm Quilts"
by Beth Donaldson
Published by EZ Quilting
by Wrights, West Warren, MA, 1997

"Contemporary Aboriginal Art:
A Guide to the Rebirth of An
Ancient Culture"
by Susan McCulloch
Allen & Unwin, Crows Nest NSW,
Australia, 1999

"Designs and Patterns from North
African Carpets & Textiles"
by Jacques Revault
Dover Publications, Inc.,
New York, NY, 1973

"Glorious Patchwork"
by Kaffe Fassett with Liza Prior Lucy
Clarkson N. Potter, Inc., New York, NY, 1997

"Guatemala Rainbow" Photographs
by Gianni Vecchiato
Pomegranate Artbooks,
San Francisco, CA, 1989

"Maya Of Guatemala – Life and Dress"
by Carmen L. Pettersen
Published by the Ixchel Textile Museum,
Guatemala City, Guatemala, 1976

"Mexican Textiles, Spirit and Style"
by Masako Takahashi
Chronicle Books LLC,
San Francisco, CA, 2003

"The Nature Of Design –
"Primitive Art"
by Franz Boas
Dover Publications, Inc.,
New York, NY, 1955

A Quilt Artist's Personal Journal"
by Joan Colvin
Fiber Studio Press, That Patchwork Place,
Bothell, WA, 1996

"The Quilter's Edge: Borders,
Bindings and Finishing Touches"

by Darlene Zimmerman
Krause Publications, an imprint of F+W Publications,
Iola, WI, 2005

"Stripes In Quilts"

by Mary Mashuta
C & T Publishing, Lafayette, CA, 1996

"Textile Arts, Multicultural Traditions"

by Margo Singer and Mary Spyrou
Davis Publications, Inc., Worcester, MA, 2000

"Textiles From Mexico"

by Chloë Sayer
University of Washington Press,
Seattle, WA, 2002

"Signs And Symbols –
African Images in African-
American Quilts"

by Maude Southwell Wahlman
Studio Books in association with
Museum of American Folk Art,
New York, NY, 1993

"Silk In Africa"

by Chris Spring and Julie Hudson
University of Washington Press,
Seattle, WA, 2002

"Symmetries of Culture, Theory and
Practice of Plane Pattern Analysis"

by Dorothy K. Washburn and Donald W. Crowe
University of Washington Press,
Seattle and London, 1988

"Threads Of Identity – Maya Costume
of the 1960s in Highland Guatemala"

by Patricia B. Altman and Caroline D. West
Fowler Museum of Cultural History, UCLA,
Los Angeles, CA, 1992

"The Textiles Of Guatemala"

by Regis Bertrand and D. Magne
Studio Editions, London, 1991

"Textiles From Guatemala"

by Ann Hecht
University of Washington Press,
Seattle, WA, 2001

"World Textiles, A Visual Guide to
Traditional Techniques"

by John Gillow and Bryan Sentence
Bulfinch Press, an imprint of Little, Brown and
Company, London, 1999

Resources

PRISCILLA BIANCHI

The Lady from Guatemala
• Workshops and Lectures
• Textile Tours to Guatemala
• One-of-a-kind art quilts, fine quality Guatemalan hand-woven textiles (retail and wholesale), kits for the projects in the book, patterns, scrap bags, great gift ideas.

Mailing address:
7801 N.W. 37th Street, Apt. 2903-GUA
Miami, FL 33166-6559
Tel: (502) 2.364.1745 in Guatemala City
Fax: (502) 2.364.2116 in Guatemala City
www.priscillabianchi.com
priscilla@priscillabianchi.com

Guatemalan Fabrics:

FABRIC BY DESIGN

17305 6th Ave. N, Plymouth, MN 55447
763-208-3878
www.fabricbydesign.net
happy@fabricbydesign.net
Unique, vibrant, beautiful fabrics; bright and whimsical Guatemalan baby quilts

INTERNATIONAL FABRIC COLLECTION

7870 West Ridge Road (Highway 20)
Fairview, PA 16415
800-462-3891
www.intfab.com
info@intfab.com
Imported cottons, dupioni silks, unusual books and patterns, sashiko supplies

NEW MOON TEXTILES

P.O. Box 40365
Pasadena, CA 91114
Tel: 626-296-6663
Fax: 626-296-6663
www.newmoontextiles.com
info@newmoontextiles.com
Authorized distributor of Priscilla Bianchi hand-woven Guatemalan textiles plus many more gorgeous fabrics for quilts, clothing, wearable art

Australia

CHANDLER'S COTTAGE CRAFTS

PO Box 7121, Beaumaris, Victoria, Australia, 3193
61-3-9589-7056

www.chandlerscottage.com
leesa@chandlerscottage.com
Decadent oriental fabrics and unique oriental-style designs, batiks and other ethnic textiles

Other ethnic, hand-made exquisite fabrics:

ART FABRIK, INC.

324 Vincent Place, Elgin, IL 60123
847-931-7684
www.artfabrik.com
laura@artfabrik.com
Beautifully hand-dyed cotton fabrics and threads, patterns, fusing books

AZABU-YA

3767 Overland Avenue
310-845-9111
www.azabu-ya.com
azabuya@earthlink.net
Open 24-7. Japanese fabric specialist

BATIK TAMBAL

10 Auburn Road, West Hartford, CT 06119
860-233-4858
www.BATIKTAMBAL.com
batiktambal@sbcglobal.net
Exquisite batik panels from Indonesia's finest batik artists

BOHEMIAN ELEMENT

206-947-1218
www.bohemianelement.com
sales@bohemianelement.com
A source of unique textiles and embellishments collected from all over the world

THE COTTON CLUB

106 N 6th - B5
208-345-5567
www.cottonclub.com
cotton@cottonclub.com
Offering quality fabric, notions, supplies around the world over 20 years! If you can't find it, we have it!

CRANBERRY FIBER ARTS

161 Bay Road (Rte.1A)
S. Hamilton, MA 01982
978-468-3871
www.cranberryfiberarts.com

helen@cranberryfiberarts.com
Non-traditional fabrics and the
finest yarns, expert service

DYENAMIC FABRICS AND DESIGNS

PO Box 765, Columbia, SC 29202
803-695-0307
www.DYEnamicFabrics.com
dyenamic4u@aol.com
Handcrafted batik cottons, rayons; private
label patterns for quilts and clothing

EQUILTER.COM

Boulder, Colorado
877-FABRIC-3 or 303-527-0856
www.equilter.com/
service@eQuilter.com
Over 20,000 products online and in stock —
2% of Sales go to Charity

FABRITIQUE

84 East Plain St., Wayland, MA 01778
508-545-1617
www.fabritique.com
info@fabritique.com
Importer of fabrics for the adventurous
quilter — exotic cottons and silks

IXCHEL MUSEUM'S GIFT SHOP

6a. Calle Final Zona 10, Campus Universidad
Francisco Marroquín
Guatemala City, Guatemala 01010
502-2-331-3739 or 502-2-331-3638
www.museoixchel.org
sbauer@museoixchel.org
Wide variety of Mayan vestures used in
Guatemala; high quality handmade handicrafts

MEKONG RIVER TEXTILES,
Susan McCauley, owner

607 Dale Drive, Silver Spring, MD 20910
301-589-1432
www.mekongrivertextiles.com
mekongtex@aol.com
Thai cotton and silk handwoven ikats and batiks, plus
clothing patterns we design for these exotic fabrics

SALSA FABRICS

Elko, Nevada, U.S.
775-577-2207
www.salsafabrics.com
chris@salsafabrics.com
Imported textiles, Kaffe Fassett lines,
and other exciting, special fabrics

SEW WHAT FABRICS
AND BATIKS ETCETERA

460 East Main St, Wytheville, VA 24382
800-228-4573
www.batiks.com
info@batiks.com
Indonesian and Malaysian batiks, cotton,
rayon, silk, and more

United Kingdom
THE AFRICAN FABRIC SHOP

19 Hebble Mount, Meltham, Holmfirth,
West Yorkshire, HD9 4HG, UK
44-1484-850188
www.africanfabric.co.uk
magie@africanfabric.co.uk
Fabrics, beads and more from all over Africa

Other Resources:
DOVER PUBLICATIONS

31 East 2nd St.
Mineola, NY 11501
516-742-5049
www.doverpublications.com
service@doverpublications.com
Over 9,000 books on art, design,
and so much more

QUILTER'S RULE INT'L, LLC

817 Mohr Ave
Waterford, WI 53185
800-242-8671
www.quiltersrule.com
customerservice@quiltersrule.com
Manufacturer of genuine Quilter's Rule,
Sewfit, Megamat and Threadbox products

QUILTWOMAN.COM

3822 Patricks Point Drive
Trinidad, CA 95570
707-677-0105; Toll free 877-454-7967
ann@quiltwoman.com
Over 150 quilt, bag and tableware patterns
from 15 international designers

RUPERT, GIBBON AND SPIDER INC.

Jacquard Products
1147 Healdsburg Ave., Healdsburg, CA 95448
Tel: 707-433-9577
Fax: 707-433-4906
www.jacquardproducts.com
service@jacquardproducts.com
Makers of quality paints and dyes for the
textile and creative artist

About the Author

Guatemalan native Priscilla Bianchi, quilt artist, designer and international teacher, represents a unique personality in today's fiber arts world. Her one-of-a-kind art quilts and wearables combine American quilt-making with the richness and ethnic appeal of Maya Guatemalan hand-woven textiles, colors, patterns and symbolism, giving life to a myriad of designs that are fresh and innovative. She lives and operates her Maya textile export business from her hometown in Guatemala City, Guatemala. Her original artwork is exhibited internationally and has been acquired by the Museum of Art & Design (formerly American Craft Museum) in New York City and many private collectors. Priscilla teaches and lectures around the world and designs fabric inspired by Guatemalan textiles for Robert Kaufman. Learn more about her innovative work, her many publications and exhibitions, her teaching schedule and her fabric lines at www.priscillabianchi.com, or contact her at priscilla@priscillabianchi.com.

Tap Into Contemporary Quilting Expertise

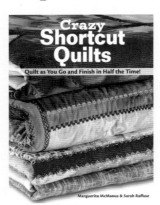

Crazy Shortcut Quilts
*Quilt as You Go
and Finish in Half the Time!*
by Marguerita McManus and Sarah Raffuse

Extend your quilting skills and passion into the limitless world of home décor, with the step-by-step instructions and 175 color photos featured in this book.

Softcover • 8¼ x 10⅞ • 128 pages
50 b&w illus. • 175 color photos
Item# Z0973 • $22.99

Quilt As Desired
*Your Guide to Straight-Line
and Free-Motion Quilting*
by Charlene C. Frable

Take your quilting skills to new heights with the six projects, using straight-line and free-motion techniques, featured in this revolutionary new guide. Discover what it means to truly quilt as desired.

Hardcover w/encased spiral binding
8¼ x 10⅞ • 128 pages
150 color photos
Item# Z0743 • $24.99

Quilting
The Complete Guide
by Darlene Zimmerman

Everything you need to know to quilt is in this book. More than 400 color photos and illustrations demonstrating the quilt making process.

Hardcover • 5⅝ x 7⅝ • 256 pages
400 color photos and illus.
Item# Z0320 • $29.99

Chameleon Quilts
*Versatile Looks
Using Traditional Patterns*
by Margrit Hall, Foreword by Earlene Fowler

Learn how to use new fabrics, colors and textures and the same set of 10 quilt patterns to create 19 different projects. Features more than 200 step-by-step color photos and graphics.

Softcover • 8¼ x 10⅞ • 128 pages
200+ color photos
Item# Z0104 • $22.99

Contemporary Quilting
*Exciting Techniques and Quilts
from Award-Winning Quilters*
by Cindy Walter and Stevii Graves

Incorporating today's hottest trends, techniques and unique methods, quilters will create 12 projects, each using the new and exciting techniques discussed. Includes a photo gallery of 75 award-winning quilts.

Softcover • 8¼ x 10⅞ • 144 pages
50 color photos. 15 illus.
Item# CNTPQ • $24.99